so take me someplace far away

CLOVER

『1』

I want happiness.

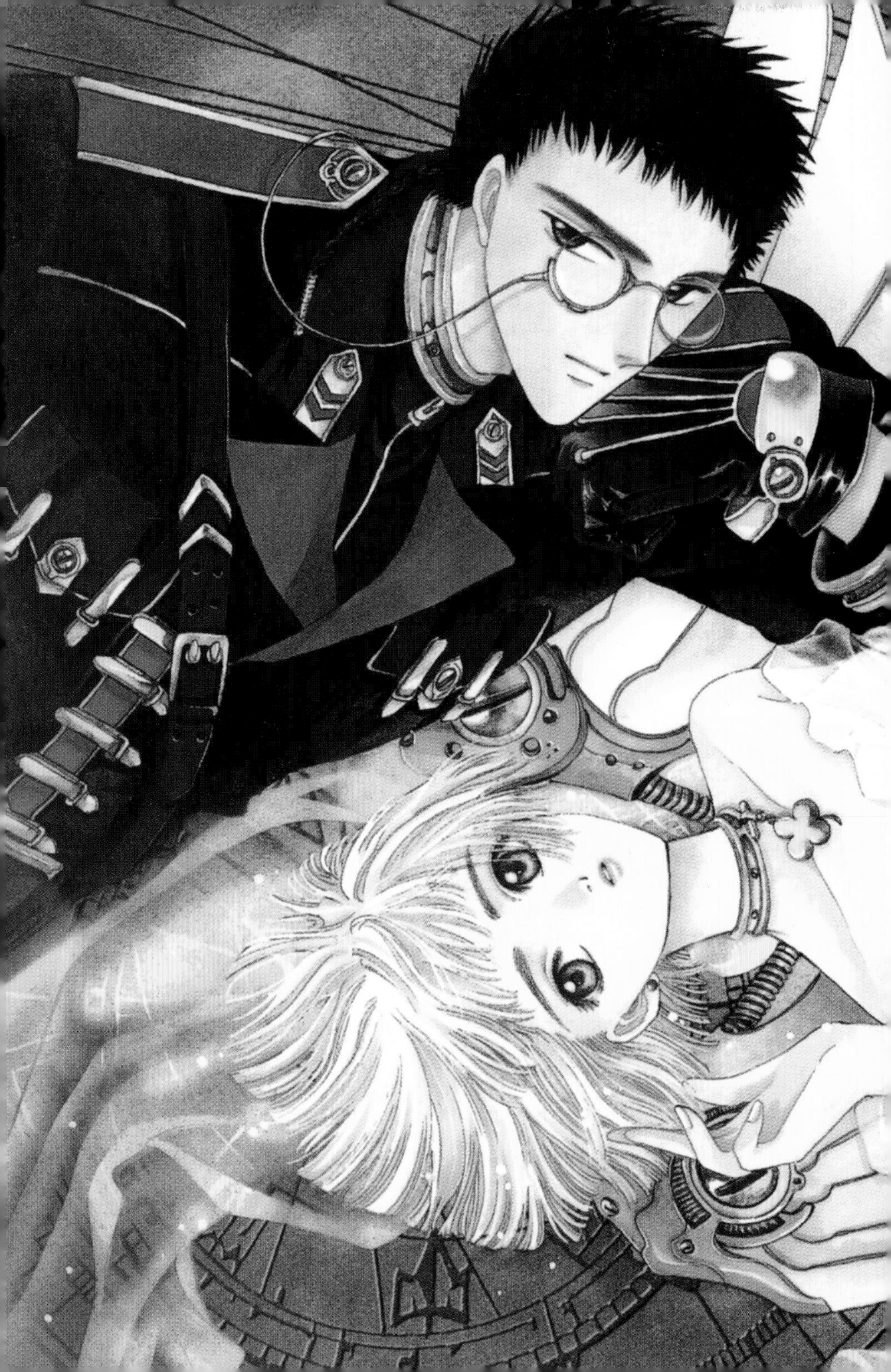

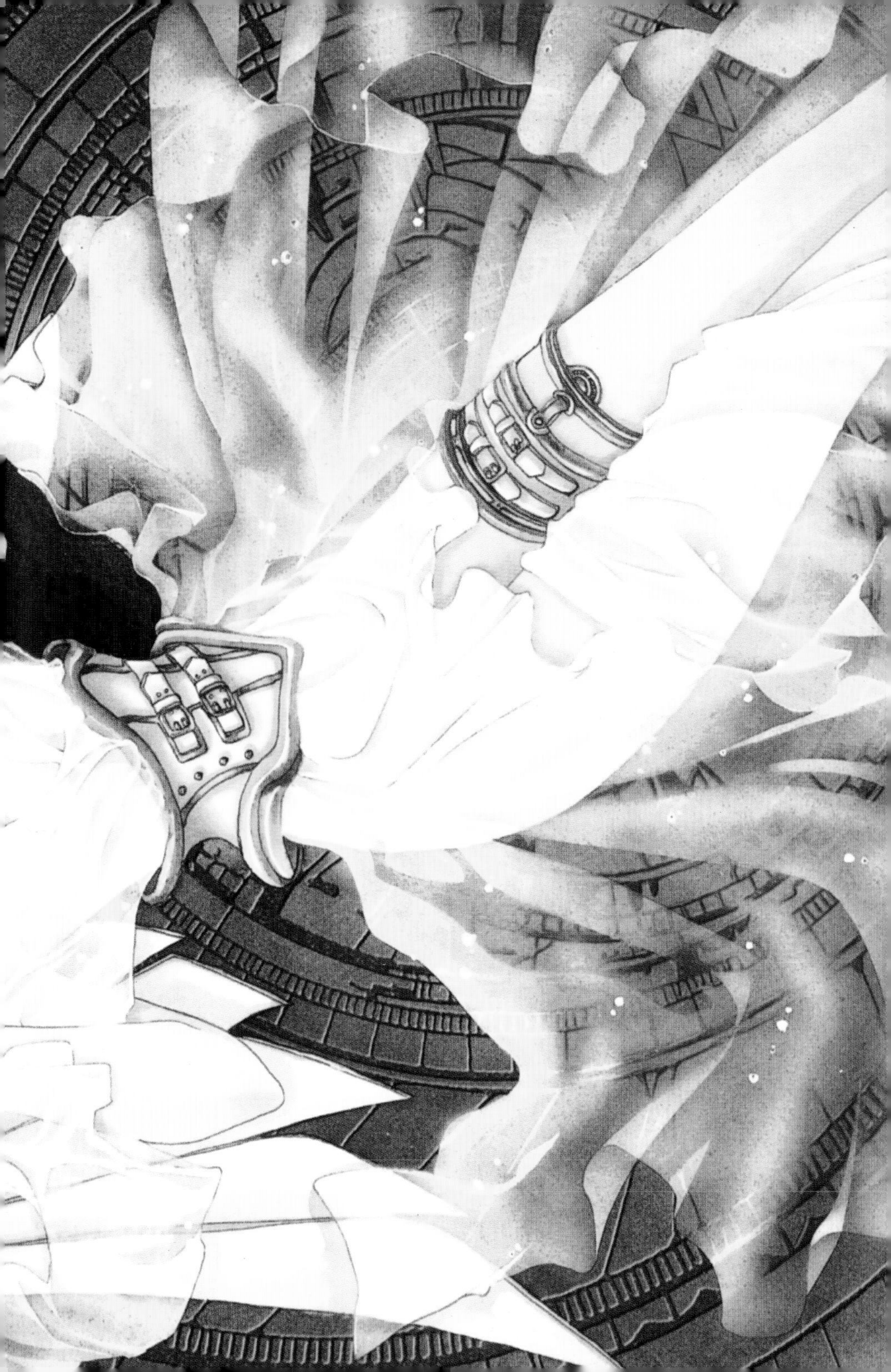

葉
leaf

森の中の小さな翼
tiny wings in the forest

歌う少女
the singing waif

鳥籠
bird cage

迷路
a maze

猫
the cat

ラジオ
a radio

跡
a trace

借り
a debt

花
a flower

議会
parliament

クローバー
clover

電話
a telephone

夜の空を飛ぶ羽のはえた魚
winged fish that flies through the night

豹
a leopard

路地裏
alleyway

傷痕
the scar

歌
a song

あるはずのない
nonexistent

おやすみ
goodnight

追跡
pursuit

羽根
feathers

They say
A four-leaf clover
brings happiness

But
Don't tell anyone

Where the clovers
Bloom white flowers

Or how many leaves
from its stem extend

A four-leaf clover

I only want your happiness
But I cannot be yours

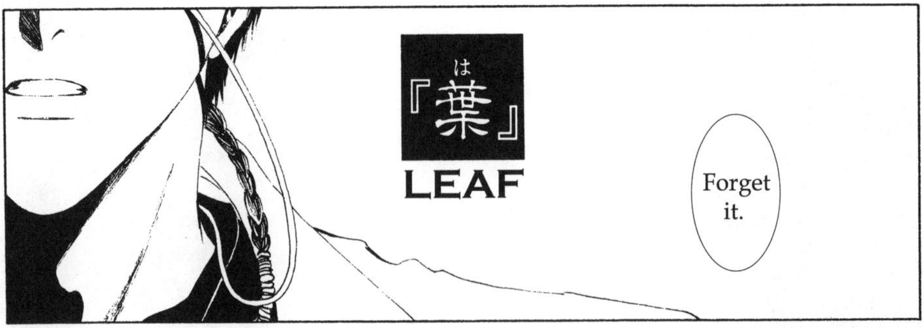
は
『葉』
LEAF
Forget it.

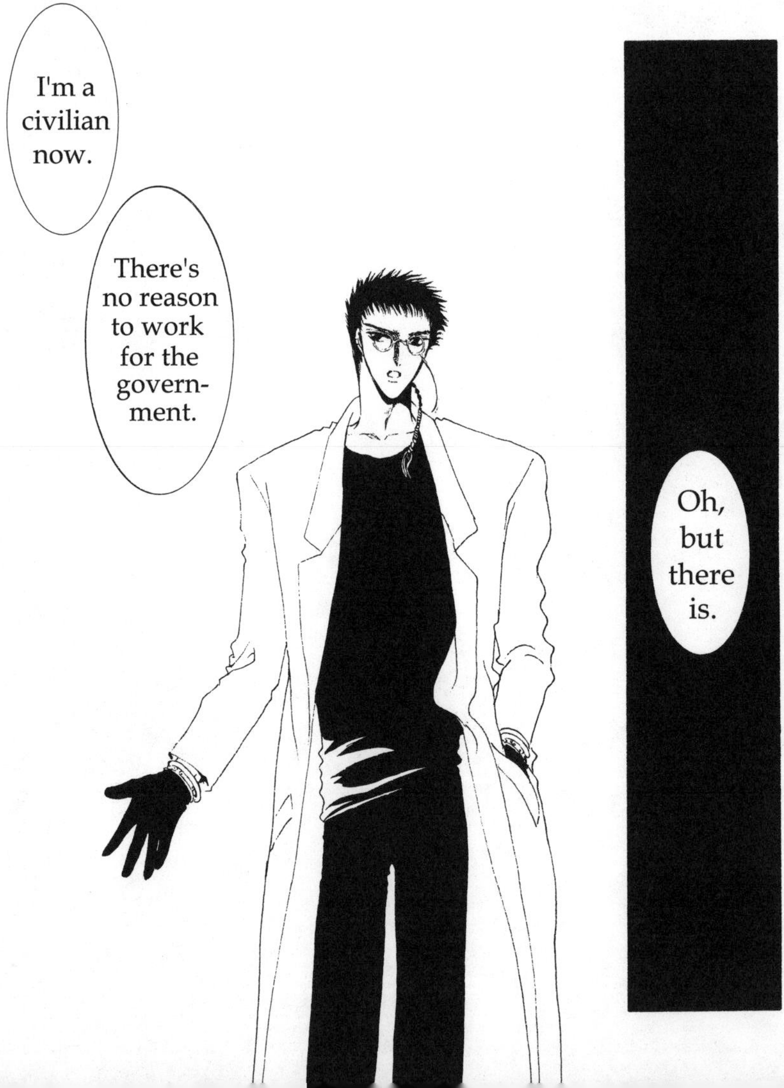
I'm a civilian now.
There's no reason to work for the govern-ment.
Oh, but there is.

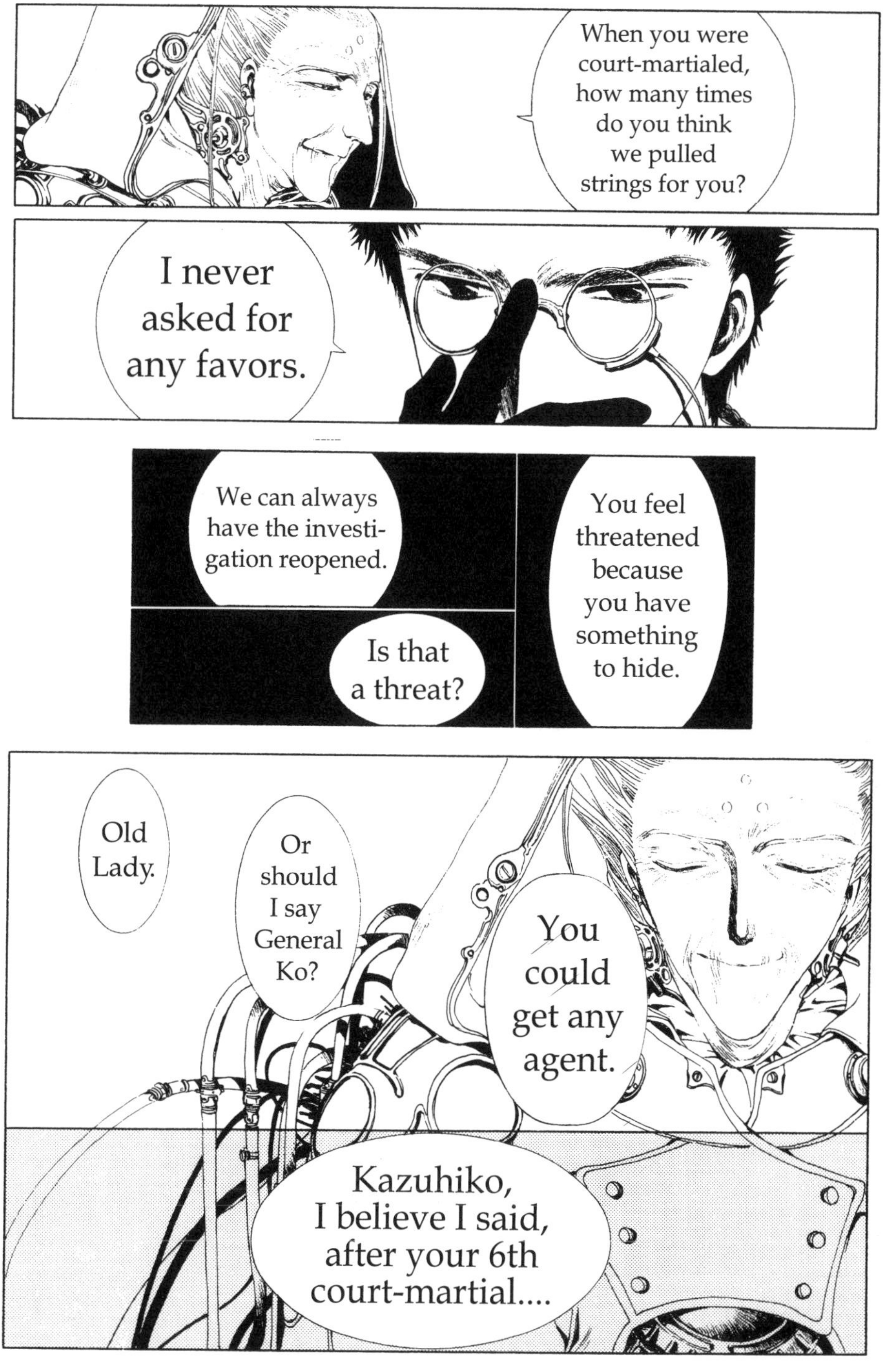
When you were court-martialed, how many times do you think we pulled strings for you?
I never asked for any favors.
We can always have the investigation reopened.
Is that a threat?
You feel threatened because you have something to hide.
Old Lady.
Or should I say General Ko?
You could get any agent.
Kazuhiko, I believe I said, after your 6th court-martial....

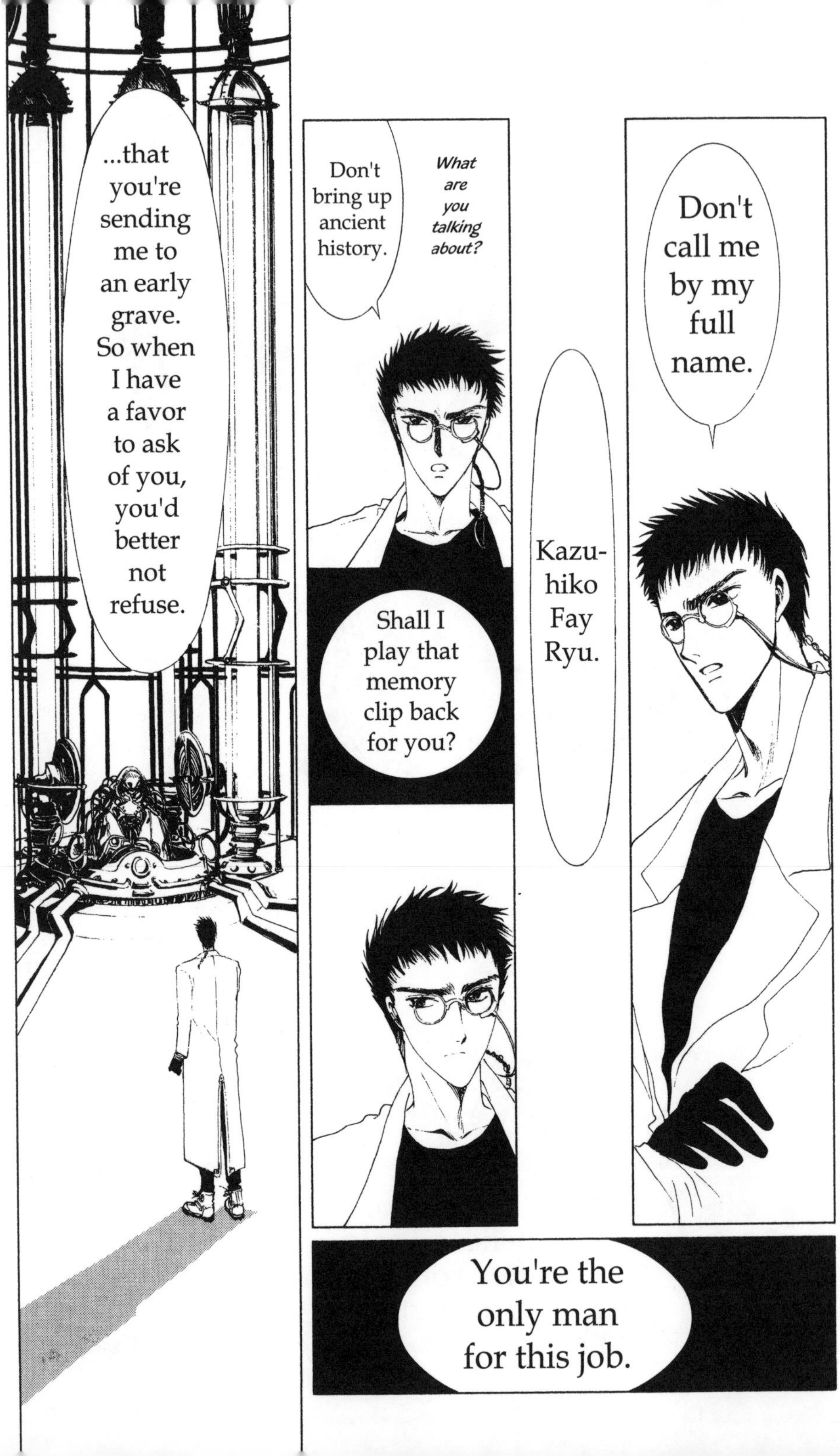
...that you're sending me to an early grave. So when I have a favor to ask of you, you'd better not refuse.
Don't bring up ancient history.
What are you talking about?
Shall I play that memory clip back for you?
Kazuhiko Fay Ryu.
Don't call me by my full name.
You're the only man for this job.

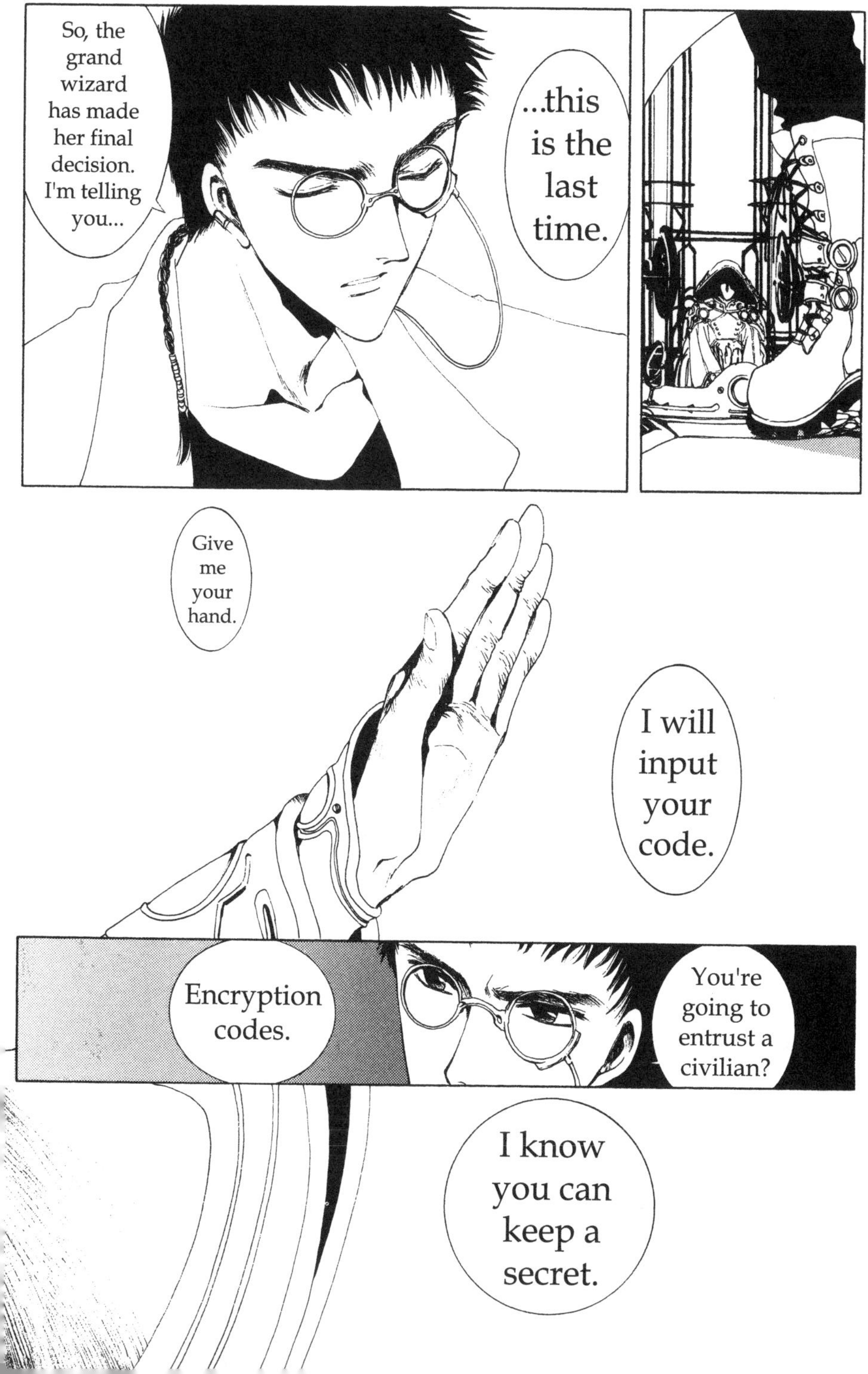
So, the grand wizard has made her final decision. I'm telling you...
...this is the last time.
Give me your hand.
I will input your code.
Encryption codes.
You're going to entrust a civilian?
I know you can keep a secret.

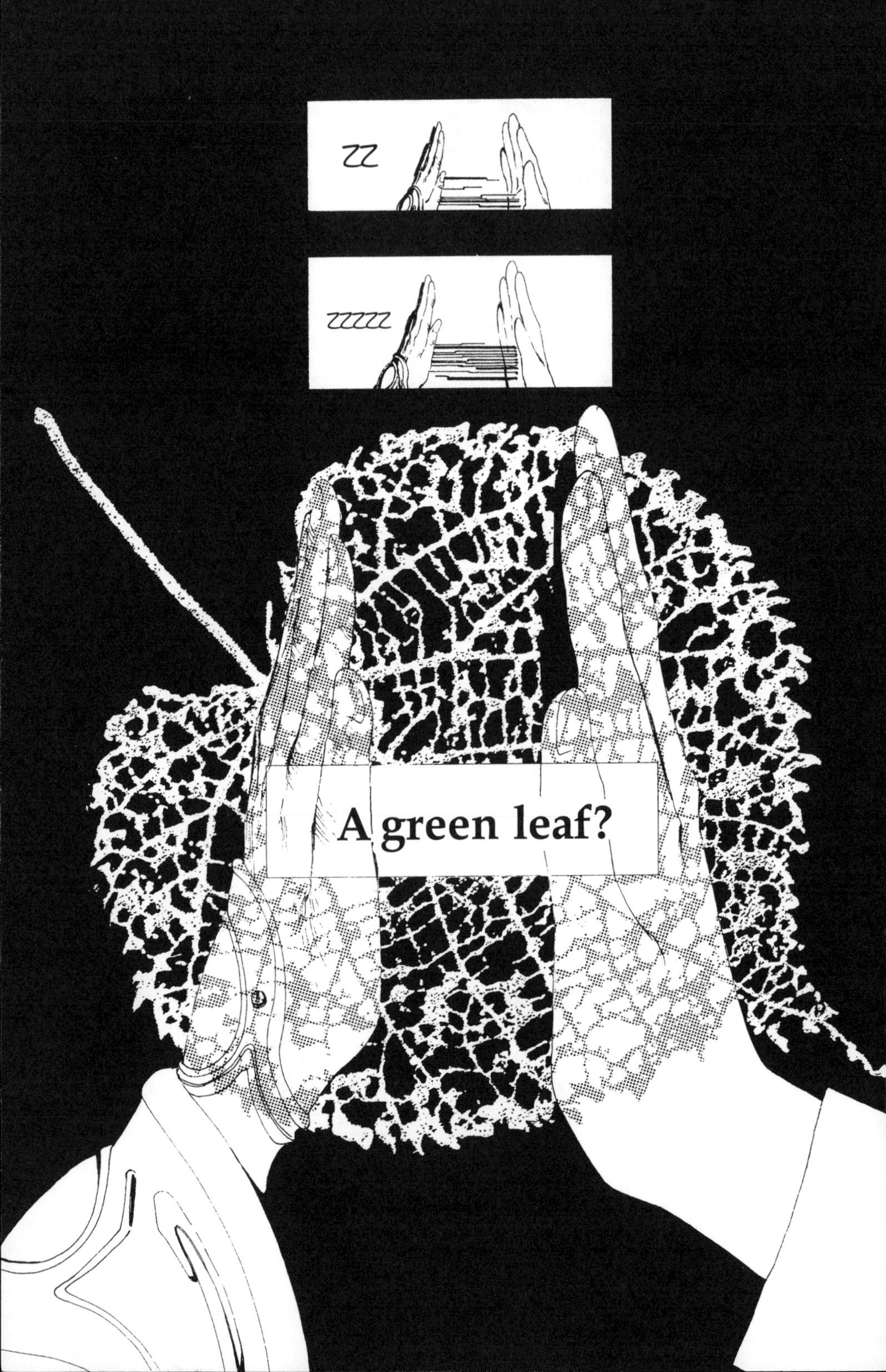
zz
zzzzz
A green leaf?

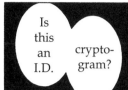

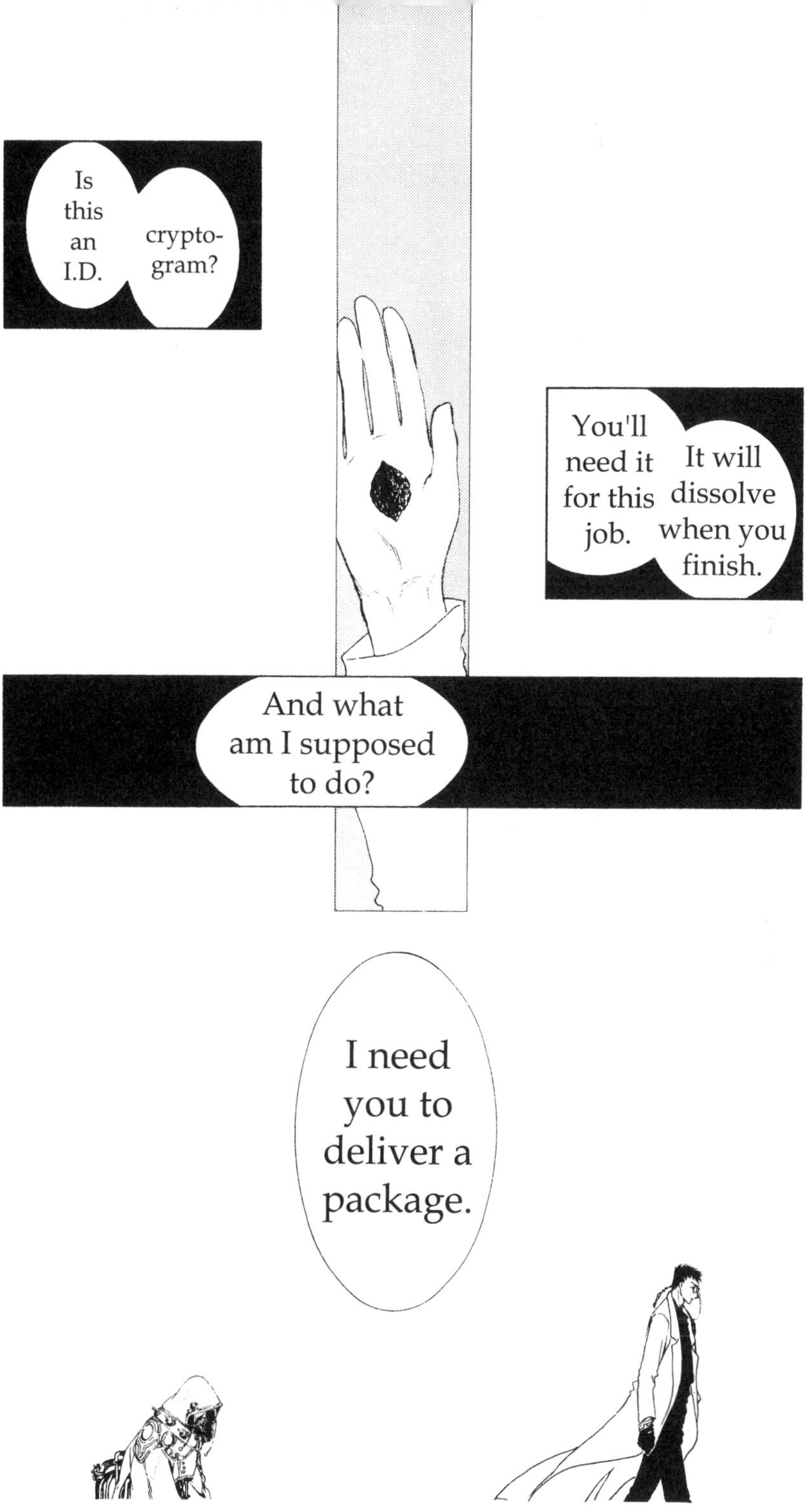

Is this an I.D.

crypto-gram?

You'll need it for this job.

It will dissolve when you finish.

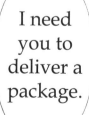

And what am I supposed to do?

I need you to deliver a package.

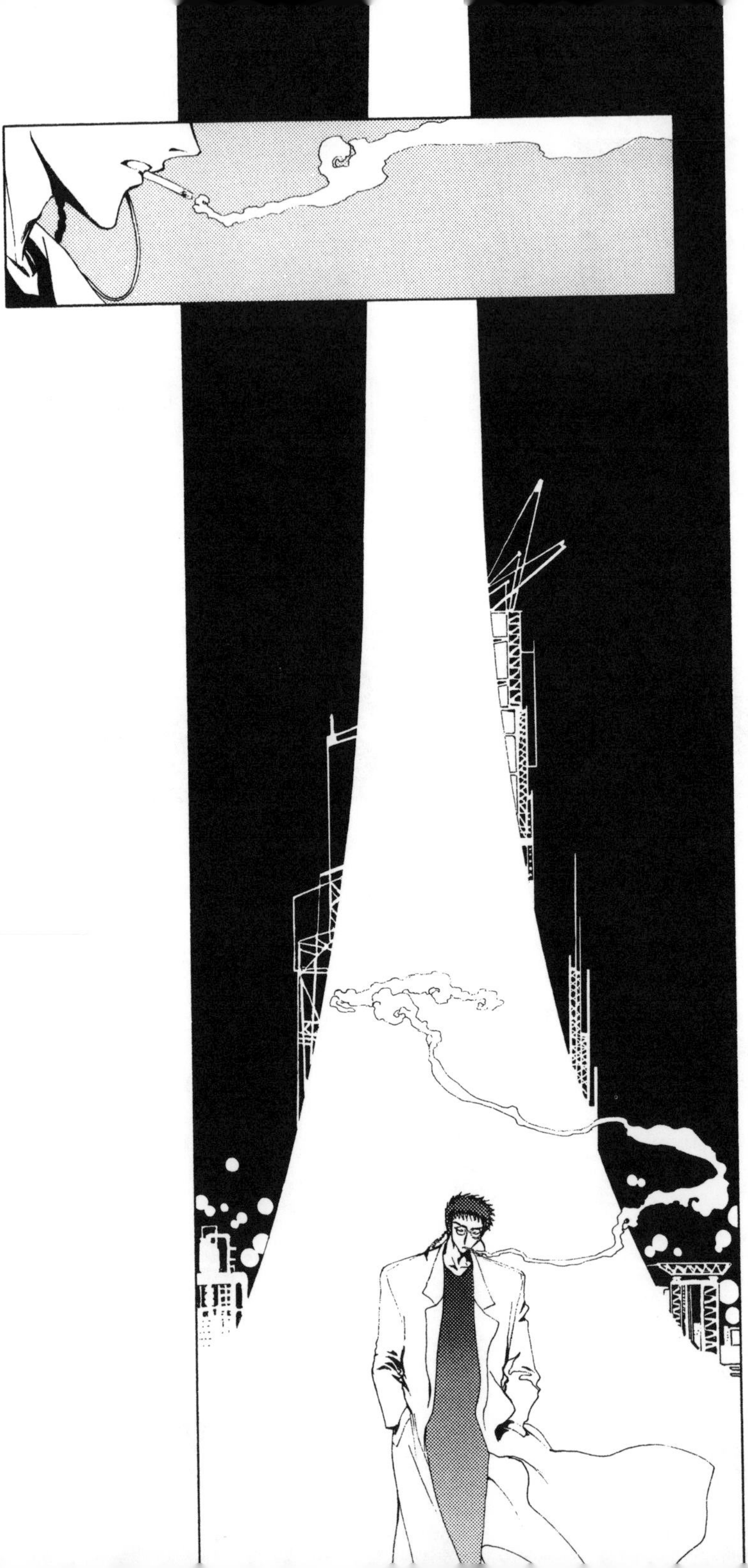

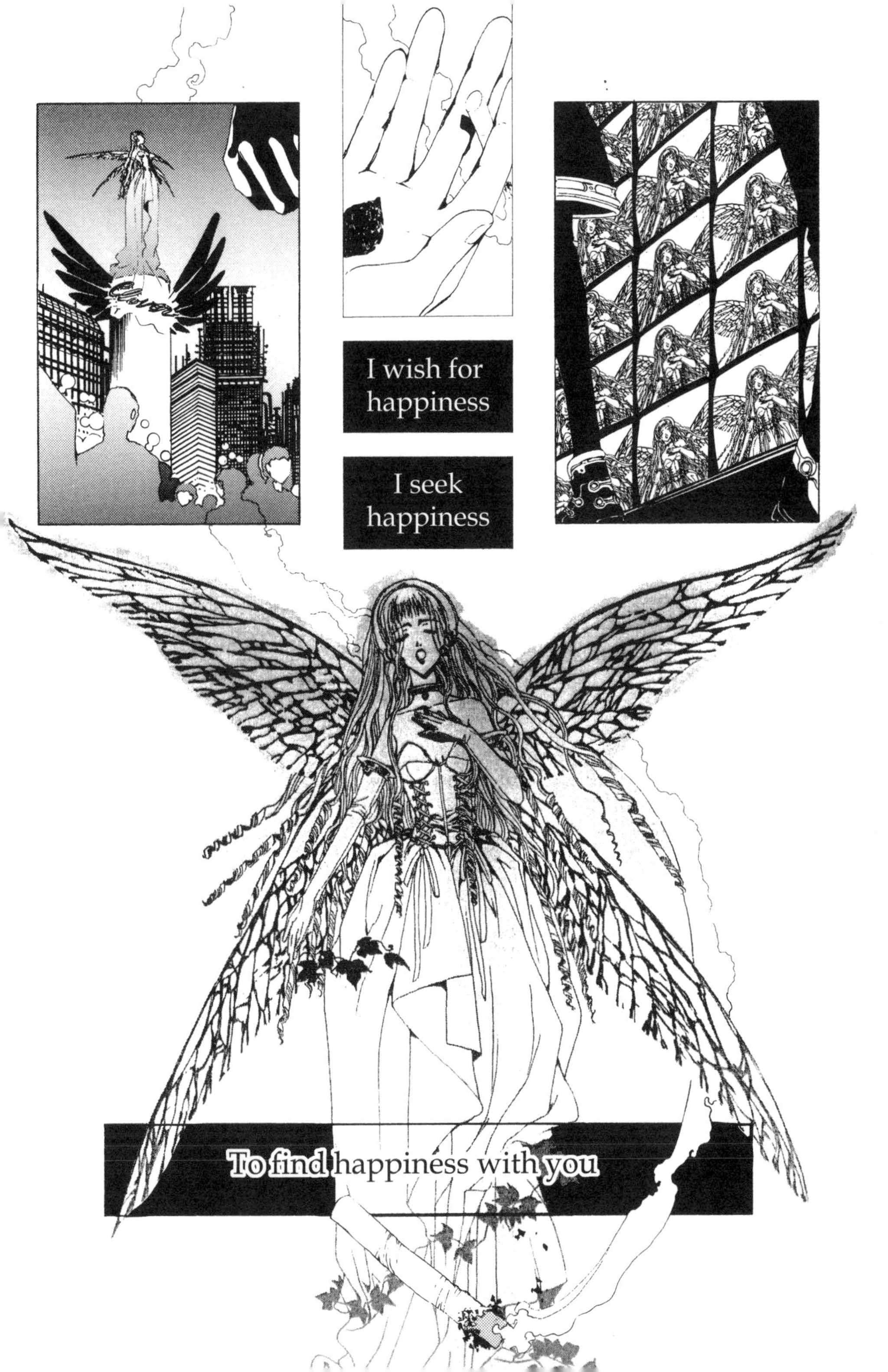
I wish for happiness
I seek happiness
To find happiness with you

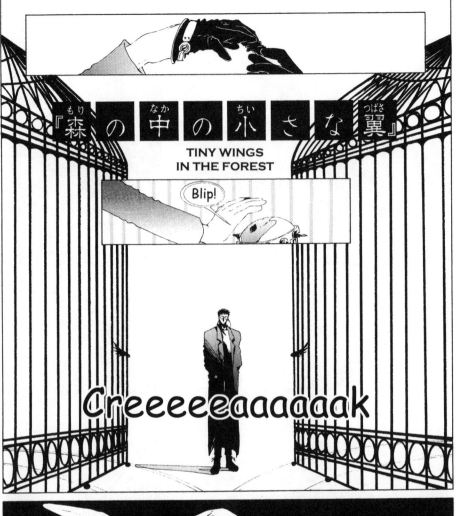

『森の中の小さな翼』
TINY WINGS IN THE FOREST

Blip!

Creeeeeaaaaaak

Welcome sir.

General Ko told us to expect you.

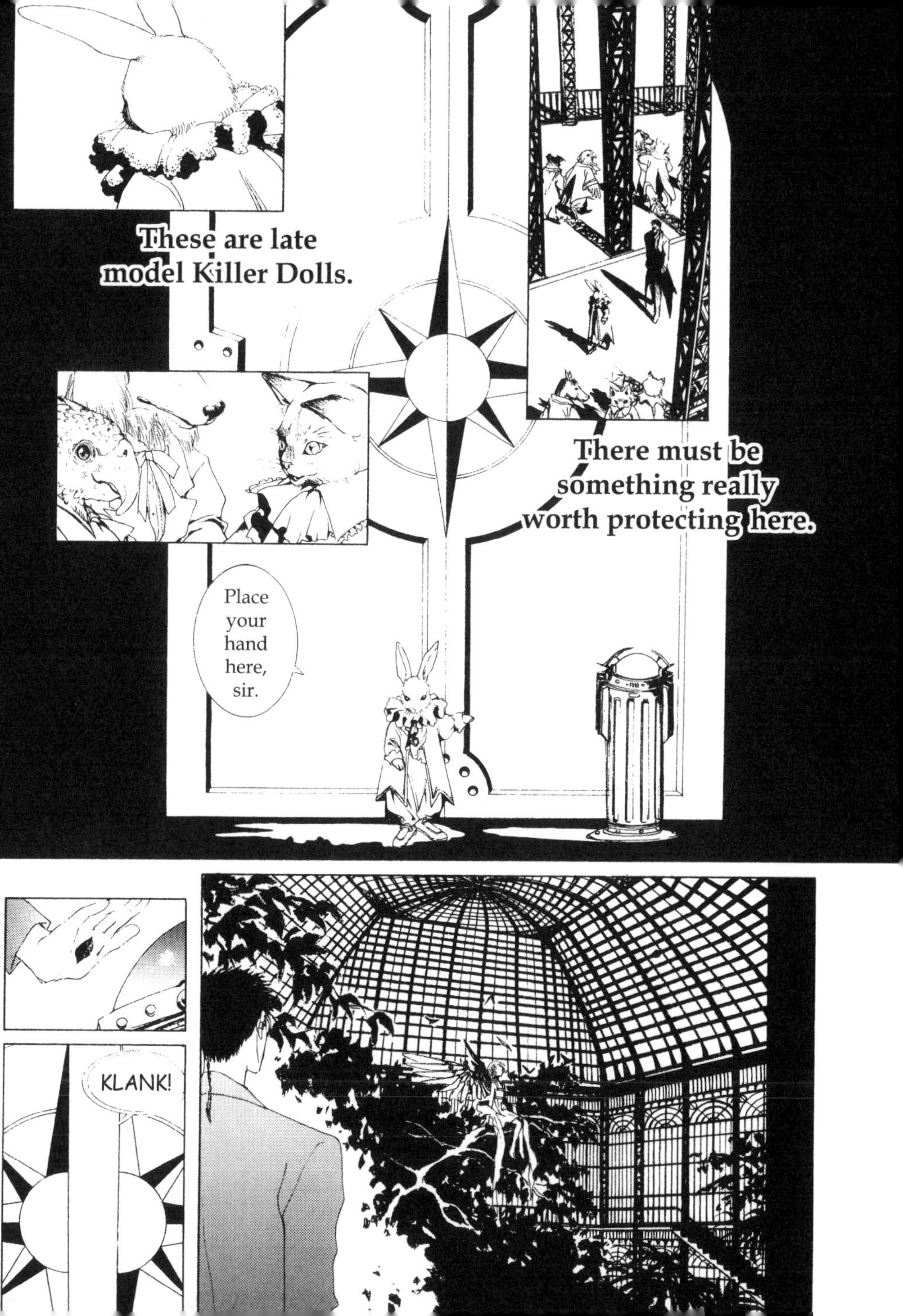
These are late model Killer Dolls.
There must be something really worth protecting here.
Place your hand here, sir.
KLANK!

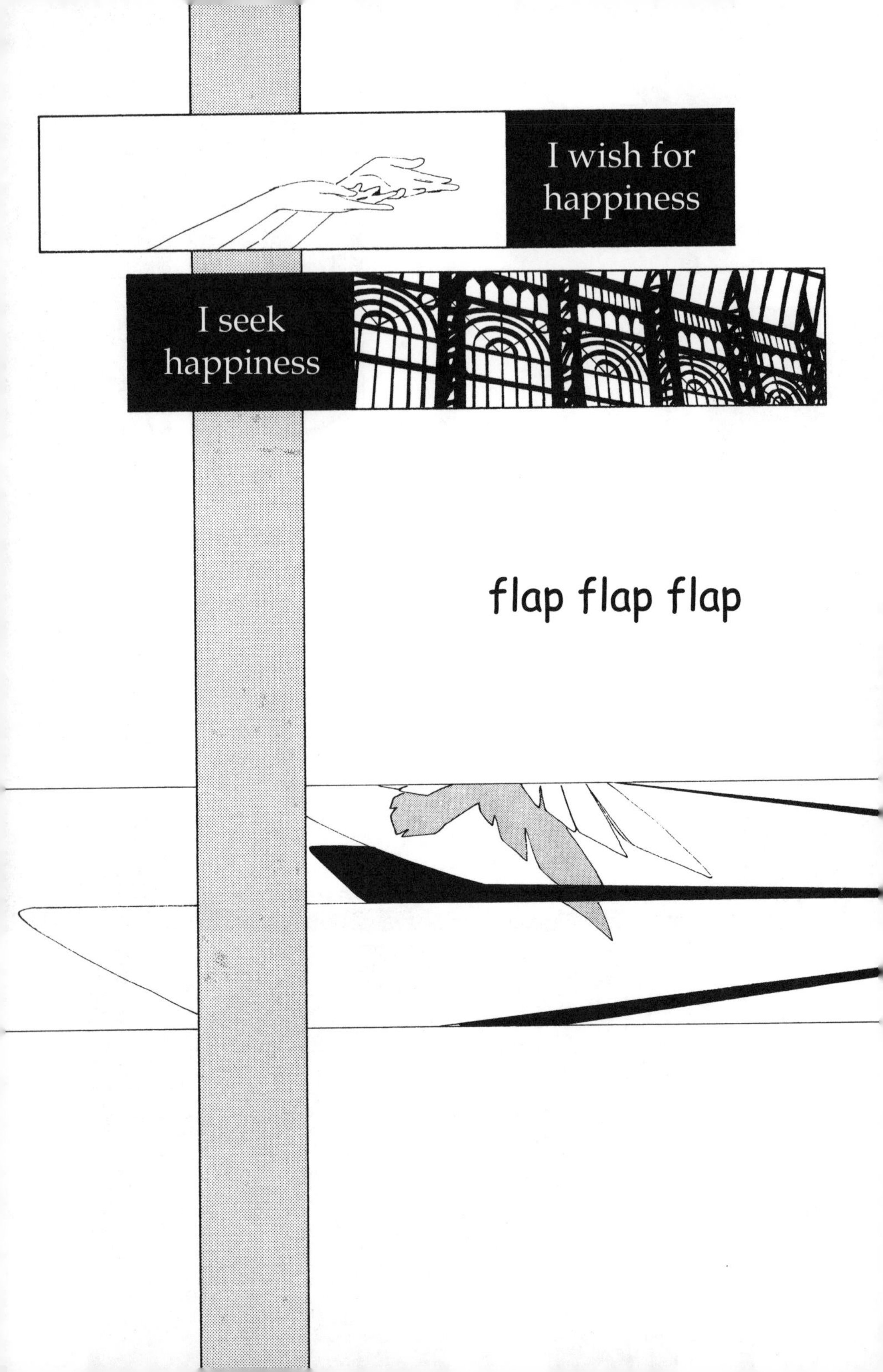
I wish for happiness
I seek happiness
flap flap flap

To find happiness
with you

To be your happiness

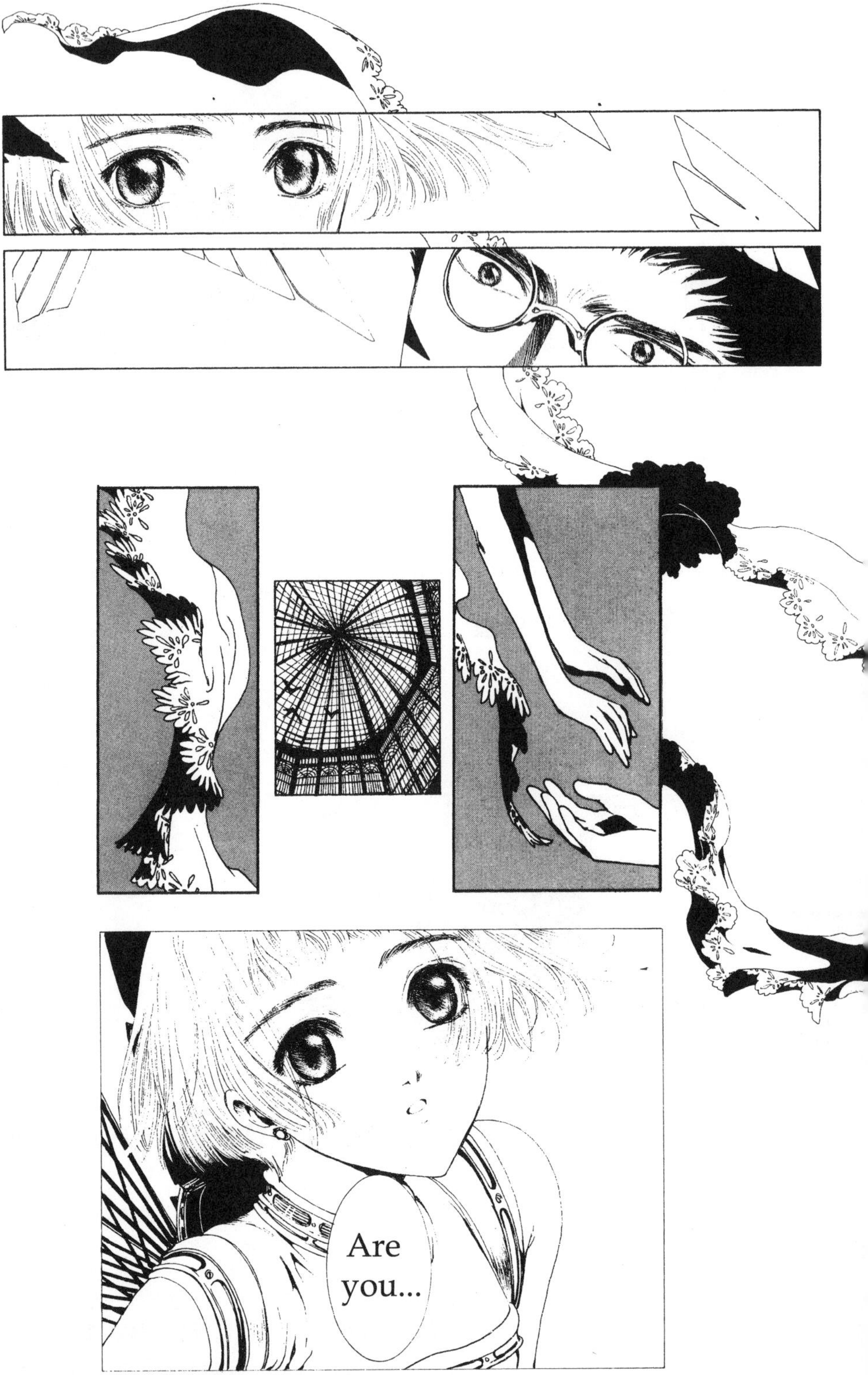
Are you...

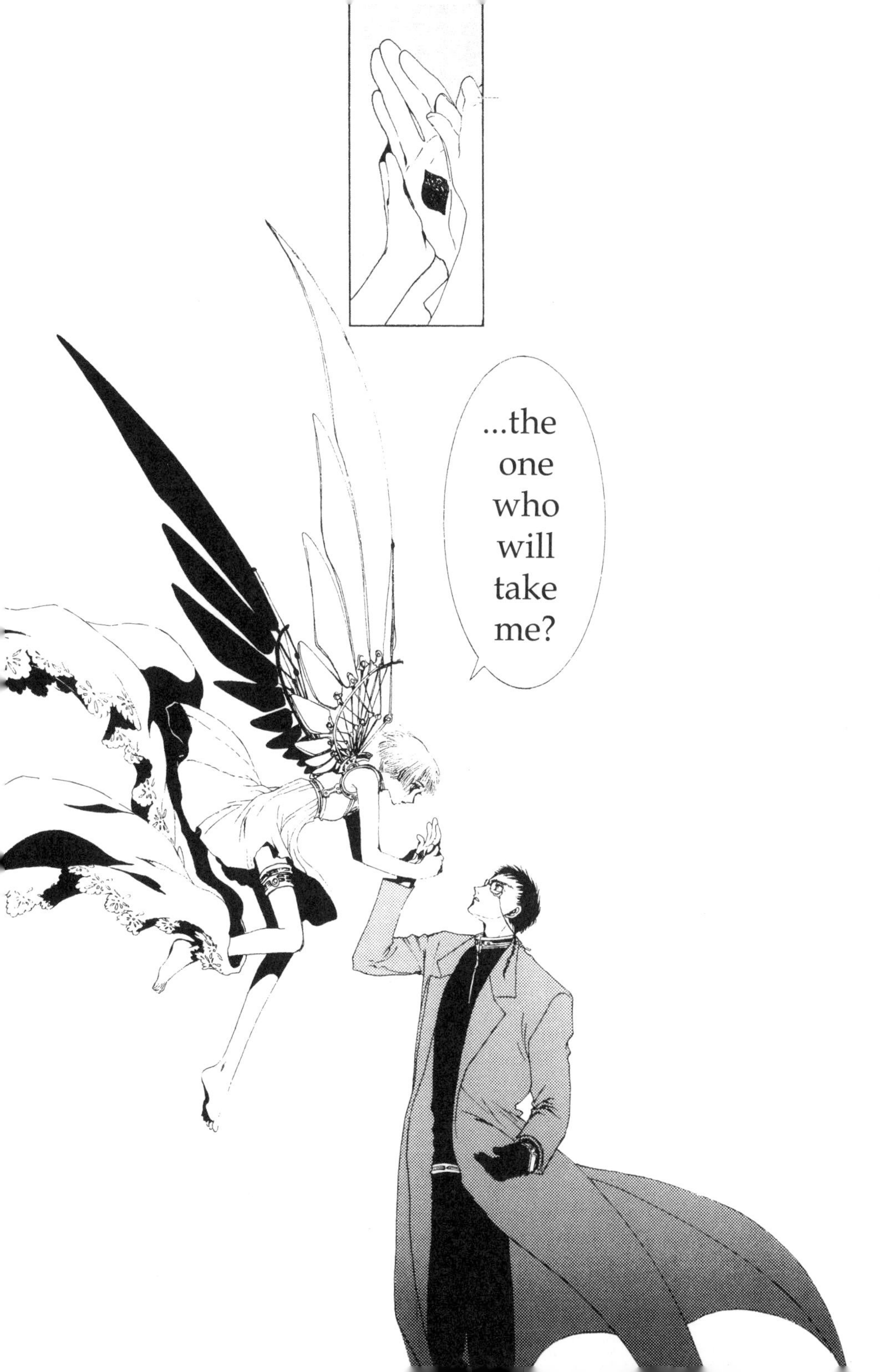
...the one who will take me?

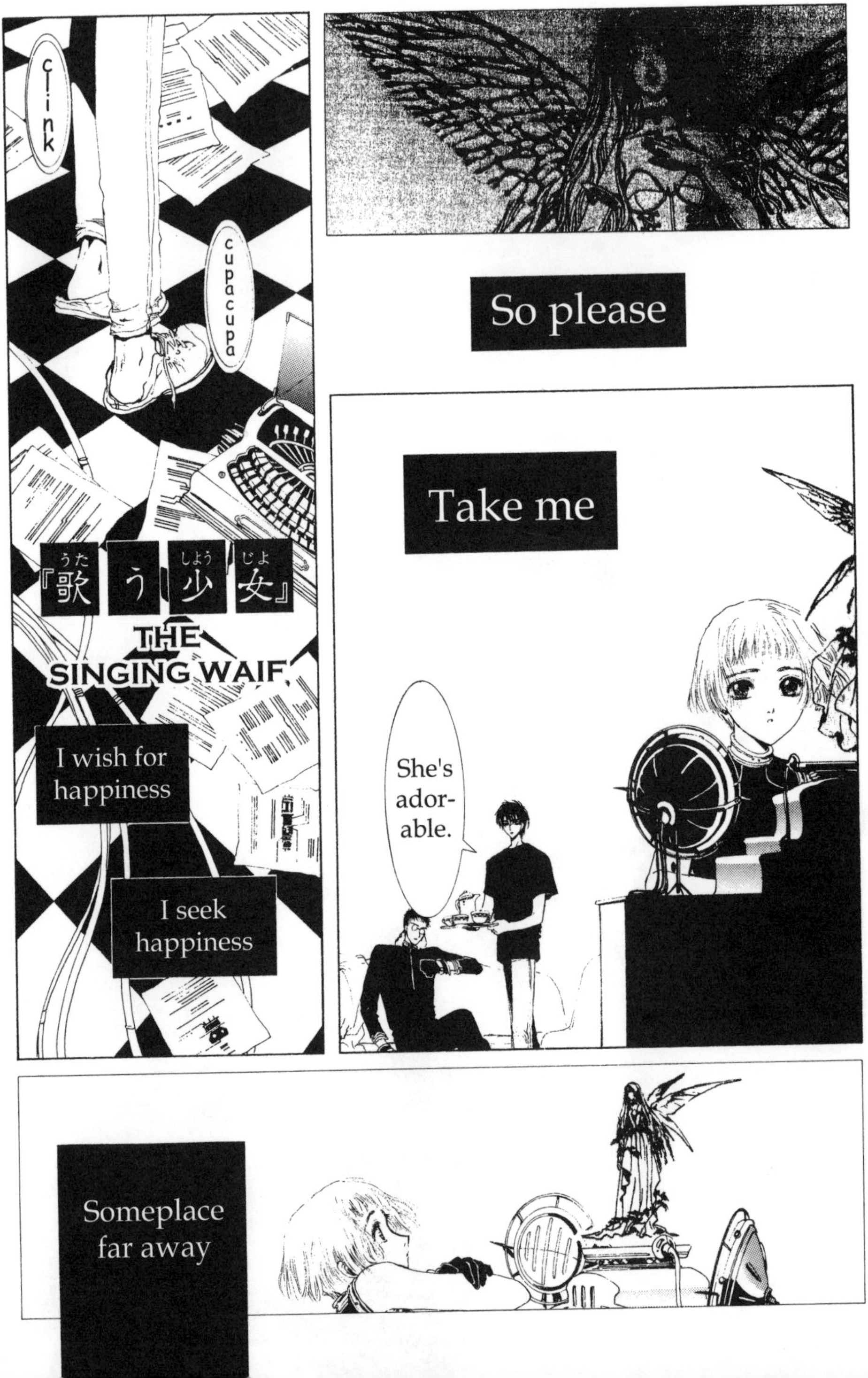
clink
cupacupa
『歌う少女』
THE SINGING WAIF
I wish for happiness
I seek happiness
So please
Take me
She's adorable.
Someplace far away

So why the change of heart?

I thought you hated kids.

How about I make you my bitch?

Run that by me again.

I said, I'll make YOU my bitch, Gingetsu.

I remember you calling Gingetsu a child molestor when he first brought me here.

You were just a kid two years ago.

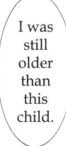

I was still older than this child.

So, who is she?

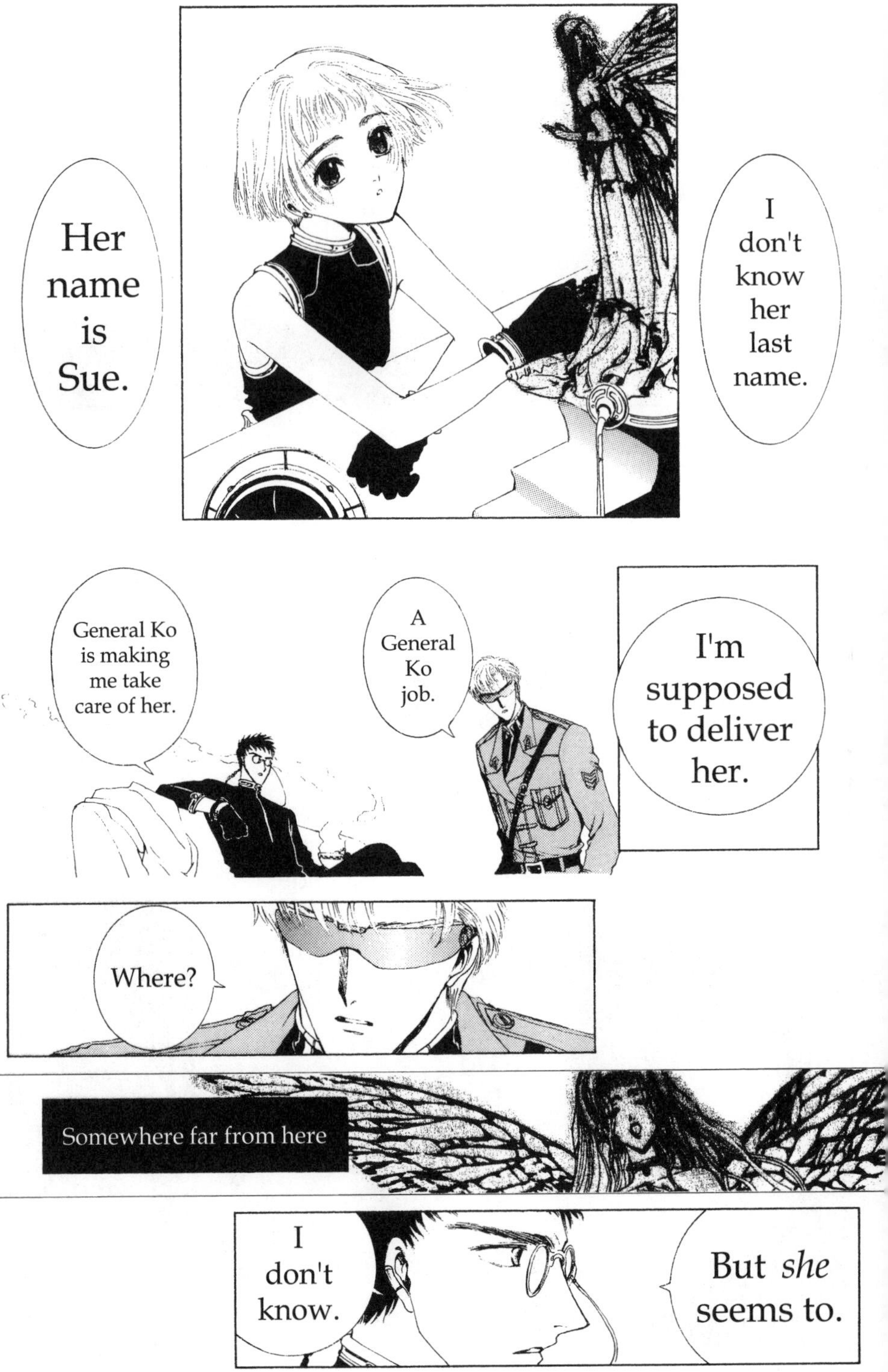
Her name is Sue.
I don't know her last name.
General Ko is making me take care of her.
A General Ko job.
I'm supposed to deliver her.
Where?
Somewhere far from here
I don't know.
But *she* seems to.

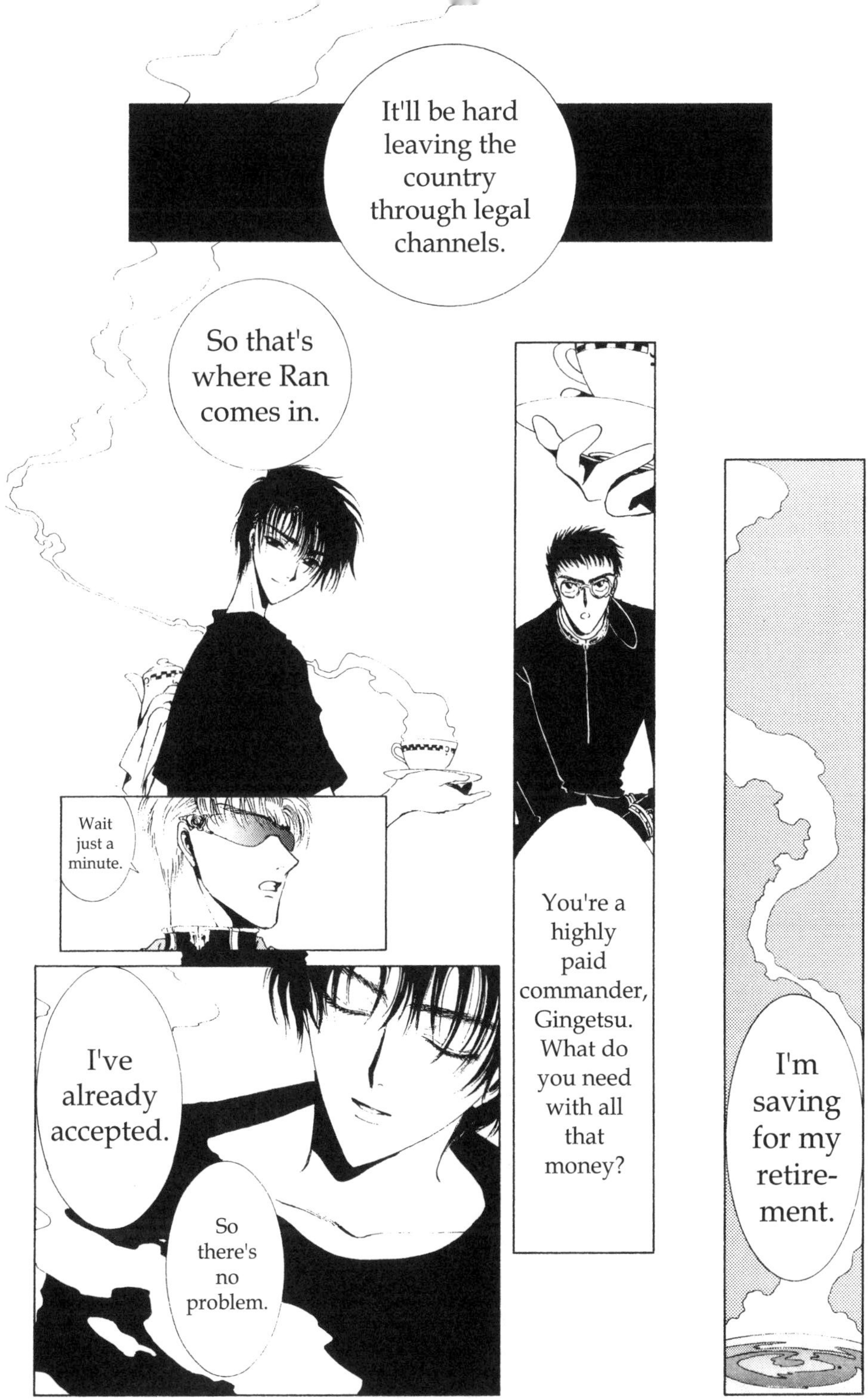
It'll be hard leaving the country through legal channels.
So that's where Ran comes in.
Wait just a minute.
I've already accepted.
So there's no problem.
You're a highly paid commander, Gingetsu. What do you need with all that money?
I'm saving for my retire-ment.

Yes.

Do you want to listen to the song again?

Click

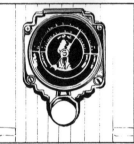

Take me away

An unbreakable spell
A never-ending kiss
An endless dream
Eternal happiness

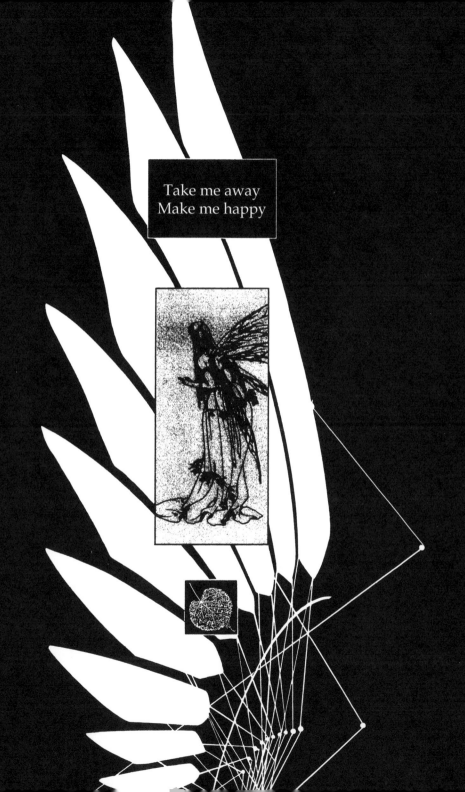

Take me away
Make me happy

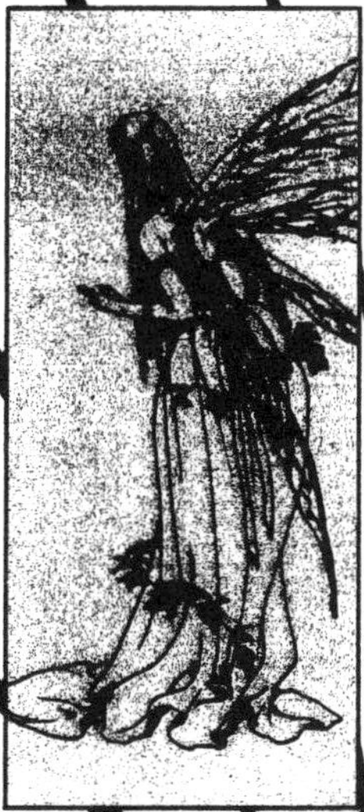

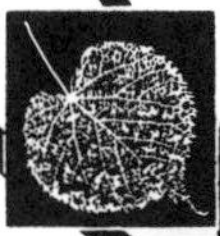

We're going to Fairy Park.

That place? It's run down.

『鳥籠』

BIRD CAGE

This transport module has been modified by...

...Ran.

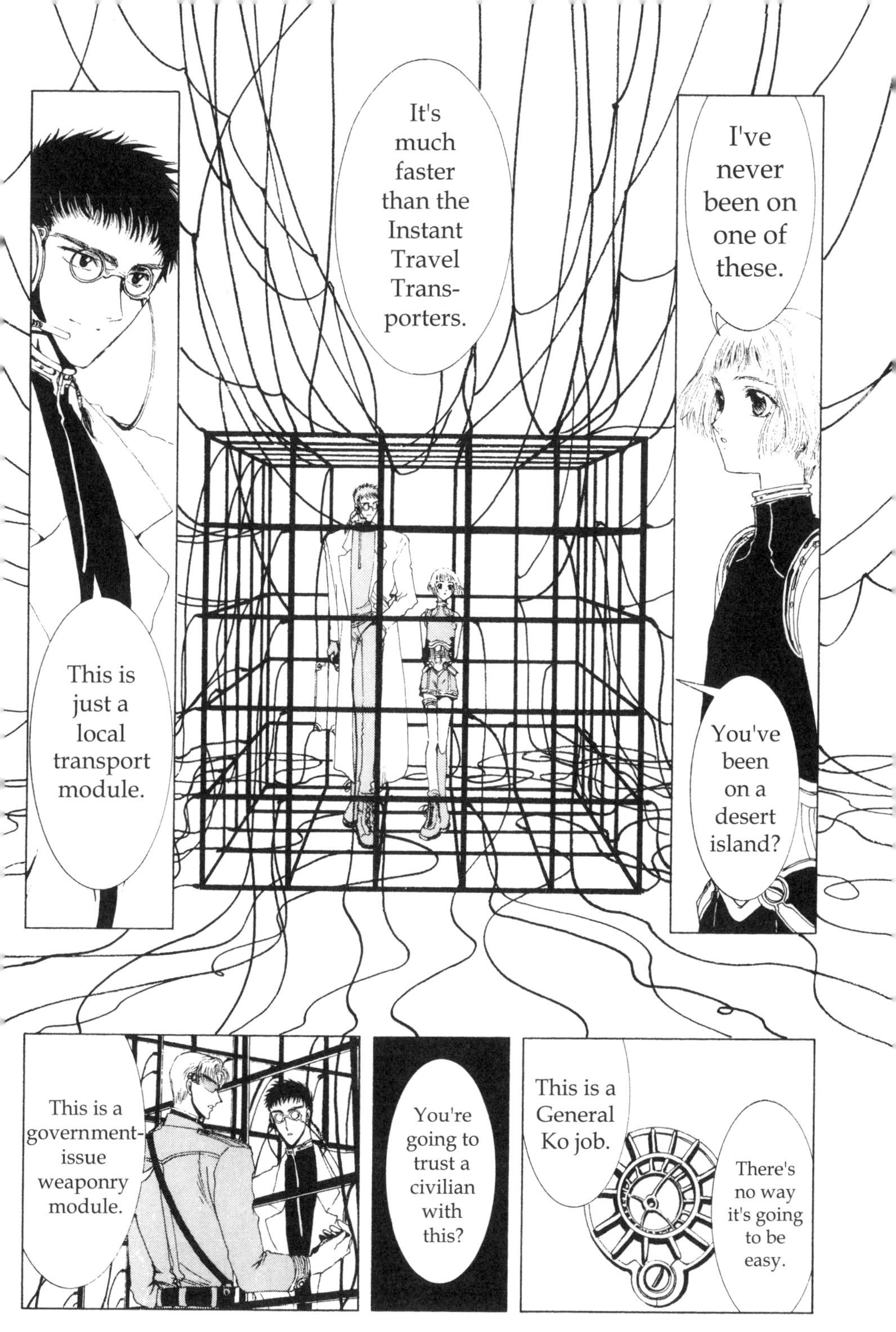
This is just a local transport module.
It's much faster than the Instant Travel Transporters.
I've never been on one of these.
You've been on a desert island?
This is a government-issue weaponry module.
You're going to trust a civilian with this?
This is a General Ko job.
There's no way it's going to be easy.

On the last job I lost my left hand. I hope this one's that easy.

Thanks. I'll take it.

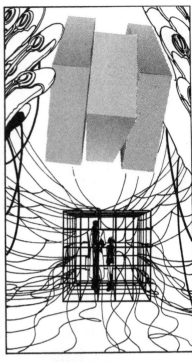

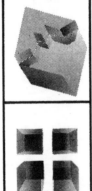

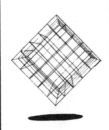

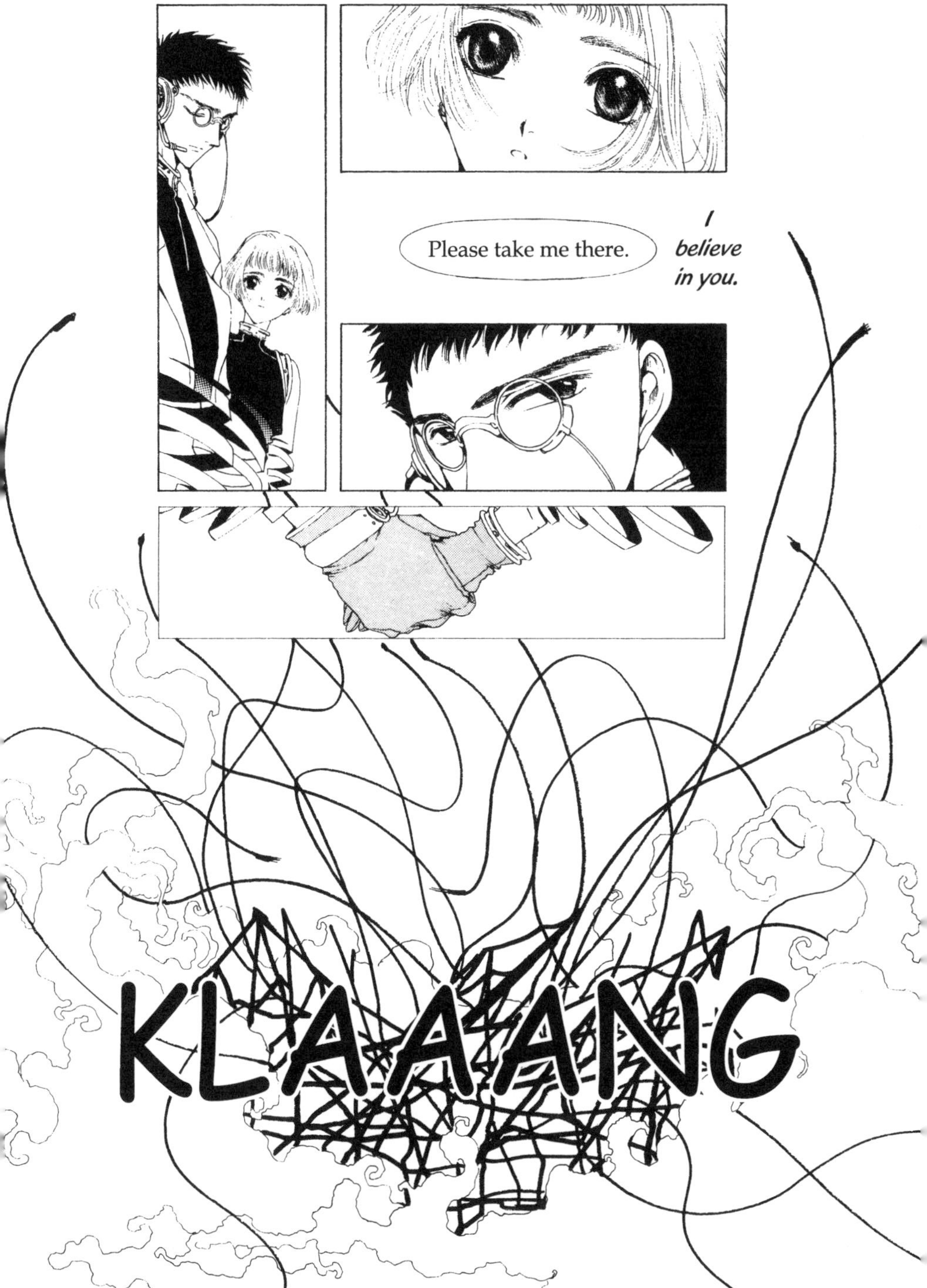
Please take me there.
I believe in you.
KLAAANG

We were intercepted.

Where did they go?

I'm searching.

Who ran that...

...interference?

I'm trying to find out.

Gingetsu...

That girl...

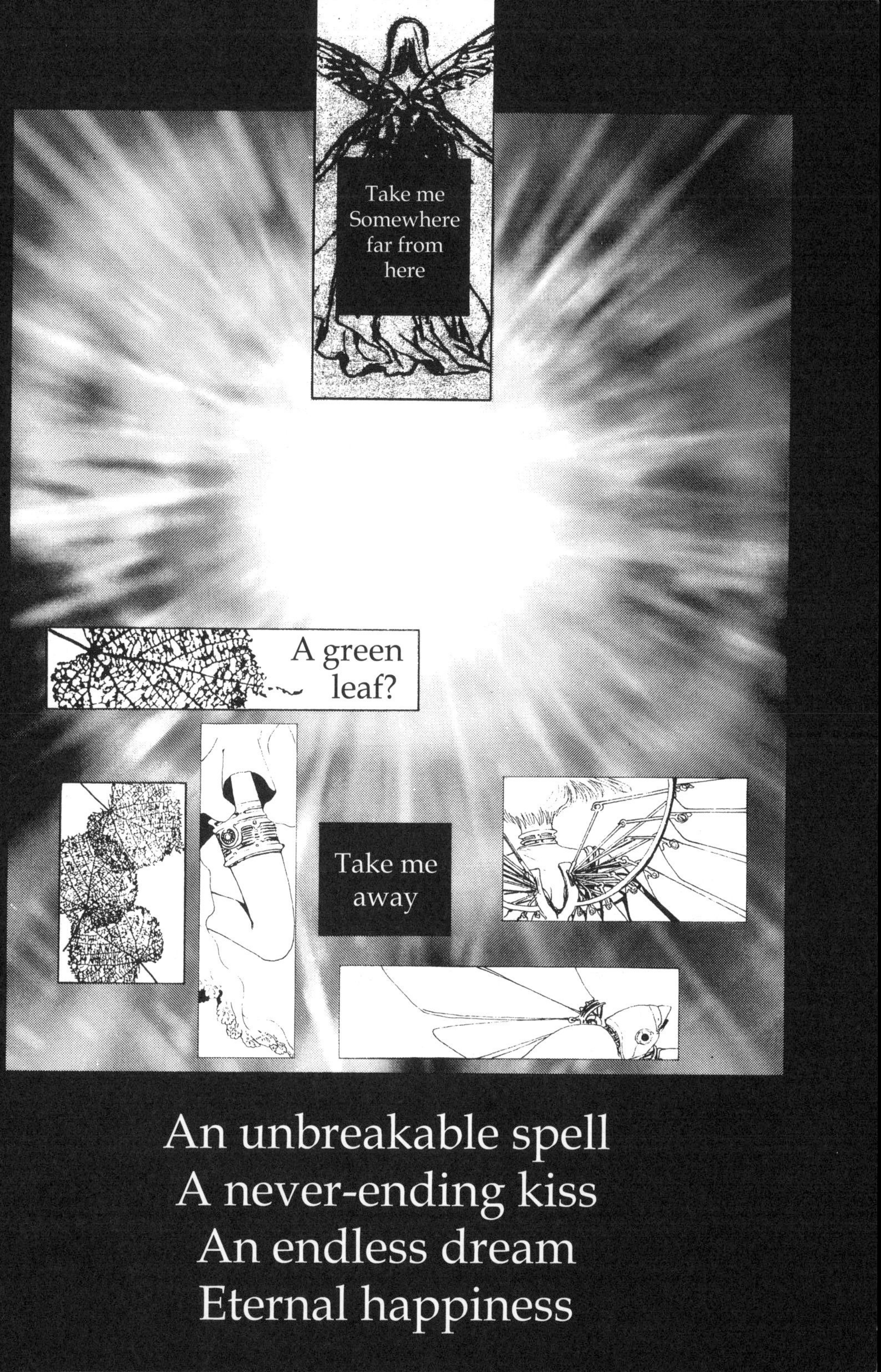
Take me Somewhere far from here
A green leaf?
Take me away

An unbreakable spell
A never-ending kiss
An endless dream
Eternal happiness

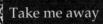

Take me away

A clover leaf?

I wish for happiness

A MAZE

『迷 路』

Is this it?

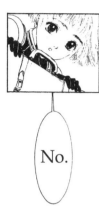

No.

Don't move.

PHFANNG

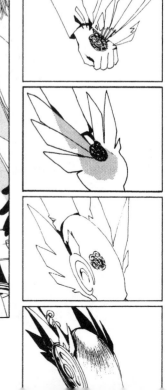

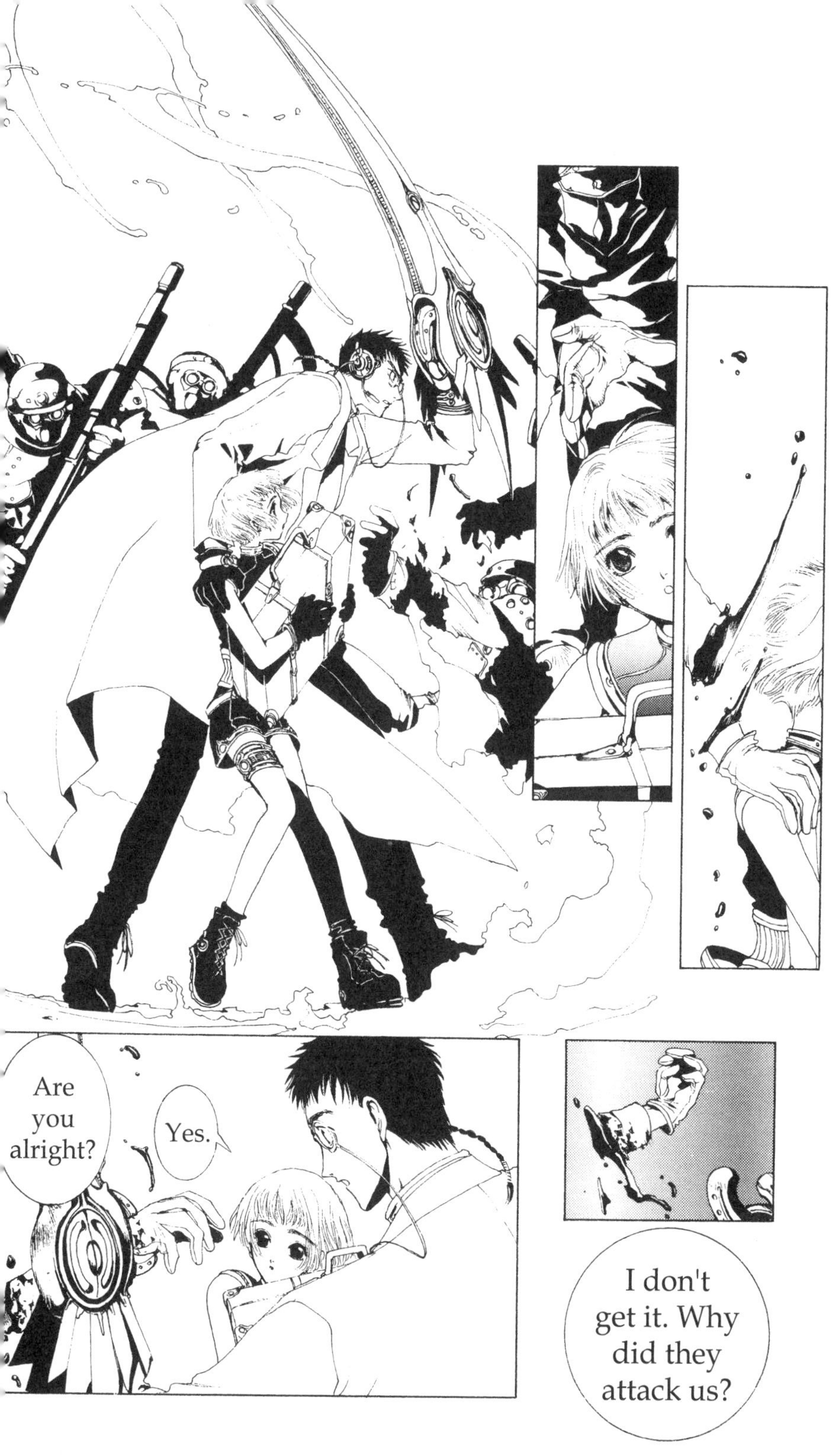
Are you alright?
Yes.
I don't get it. Why did they attack us?

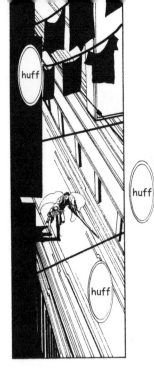

huff
huff
huff
Do you want me to carry that?
No, I'm alright.
Your hand...
Don't worry.
It's artifi-cial.
These military issues are top quality.
ZZZZZZZ ZZZZZZZ ZZZZZZZ
I can't get a clear signal.
tap

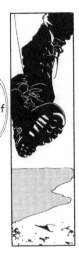

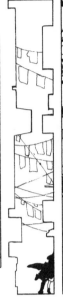

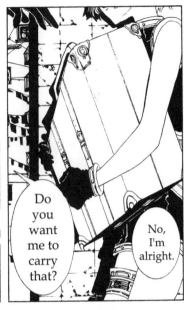

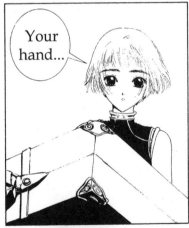

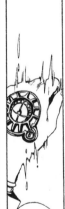

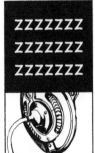

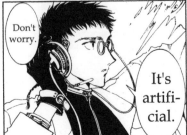

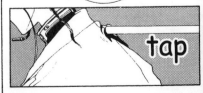

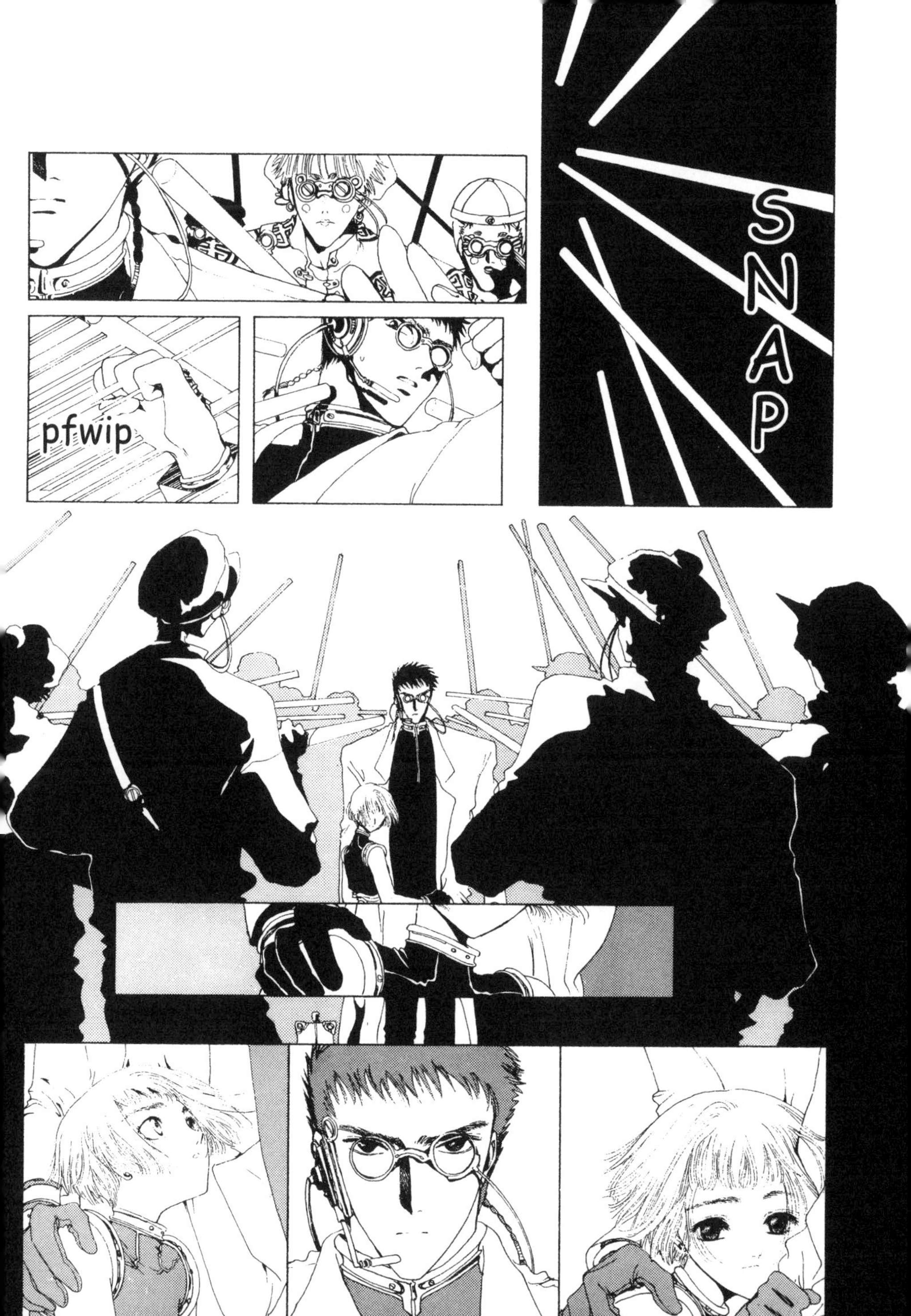
pfwip
SNAP

THE CAT

『猫』

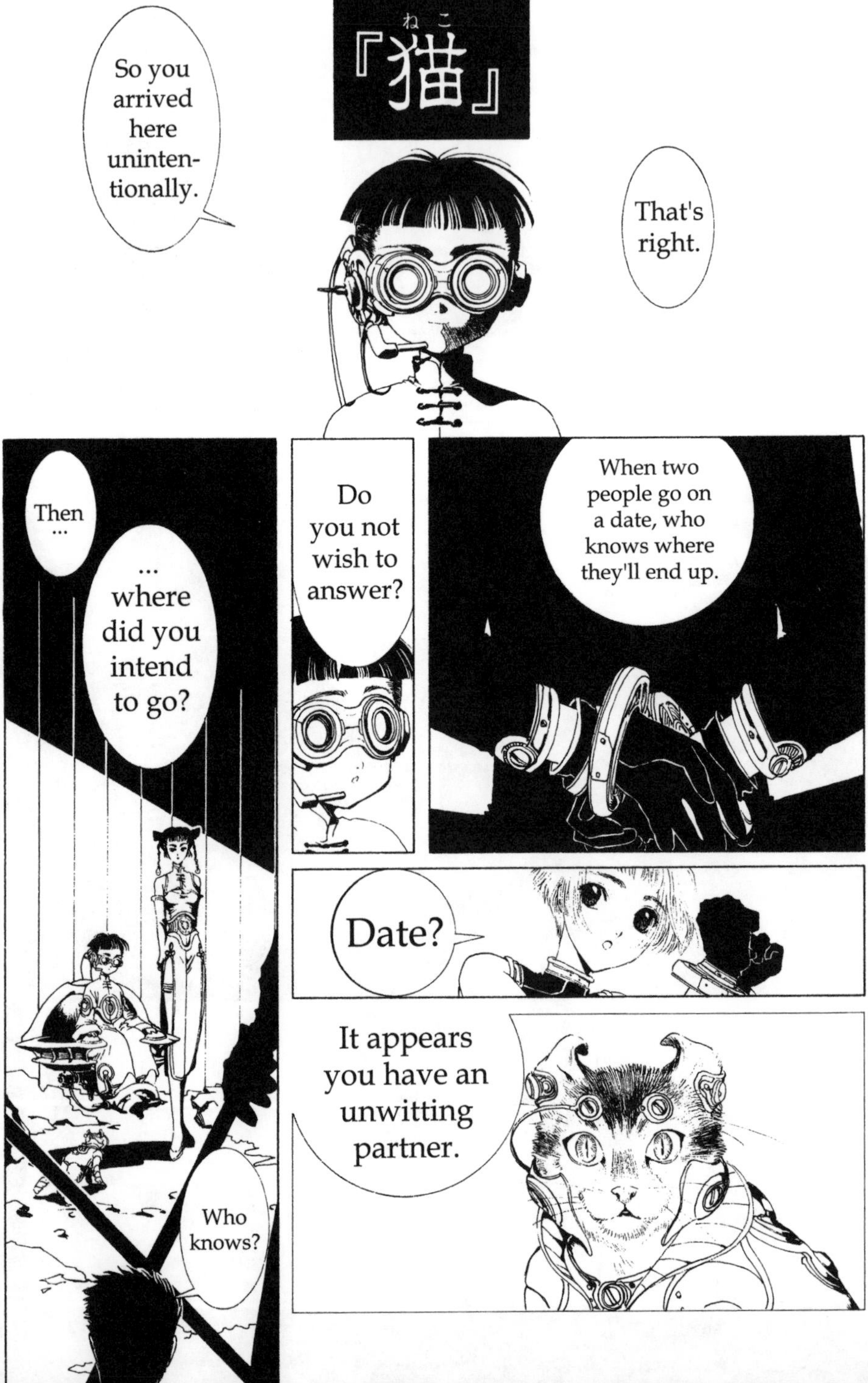

So you arrived here unintentionally.
That's right.
Then ...
... where did you intend to go?
Who knows?
Do you not wish to answer?
When two people go on a date, who knows where they'll end up.
Date?
It appears you have an unwitting partner.

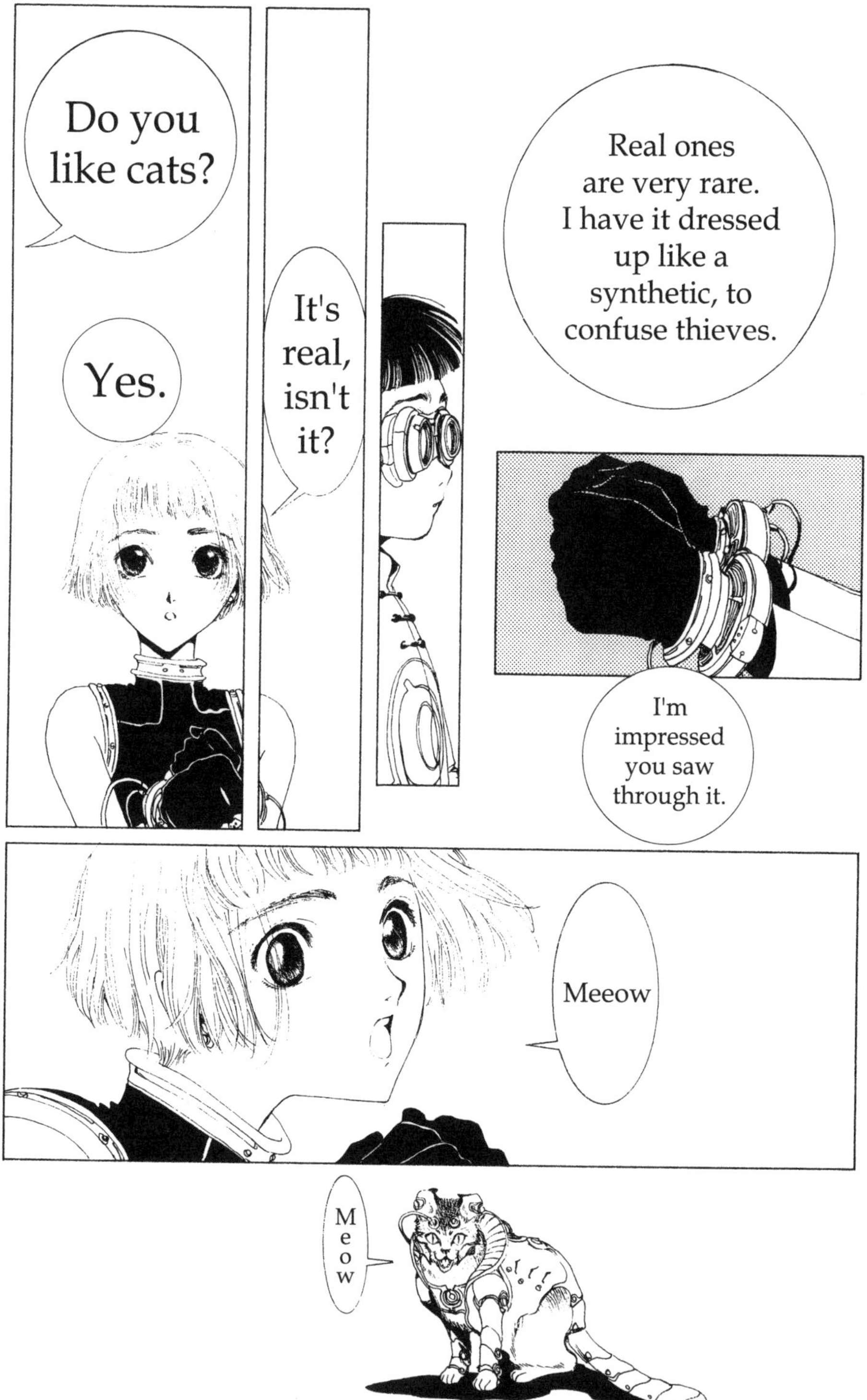
Do you like cats?
Yes.
It's real, isn't it?
Real ones are very rare. I have it dressed up like a synthetic, to confuse thieves.
I'm impressed you saw through it.
Meeow
Meow

You will be our guests while we investigate further.

Tao Fa...

Please show our guests their rooms.

We're in kind of a hurry.

『ラジオ』

A RADIO

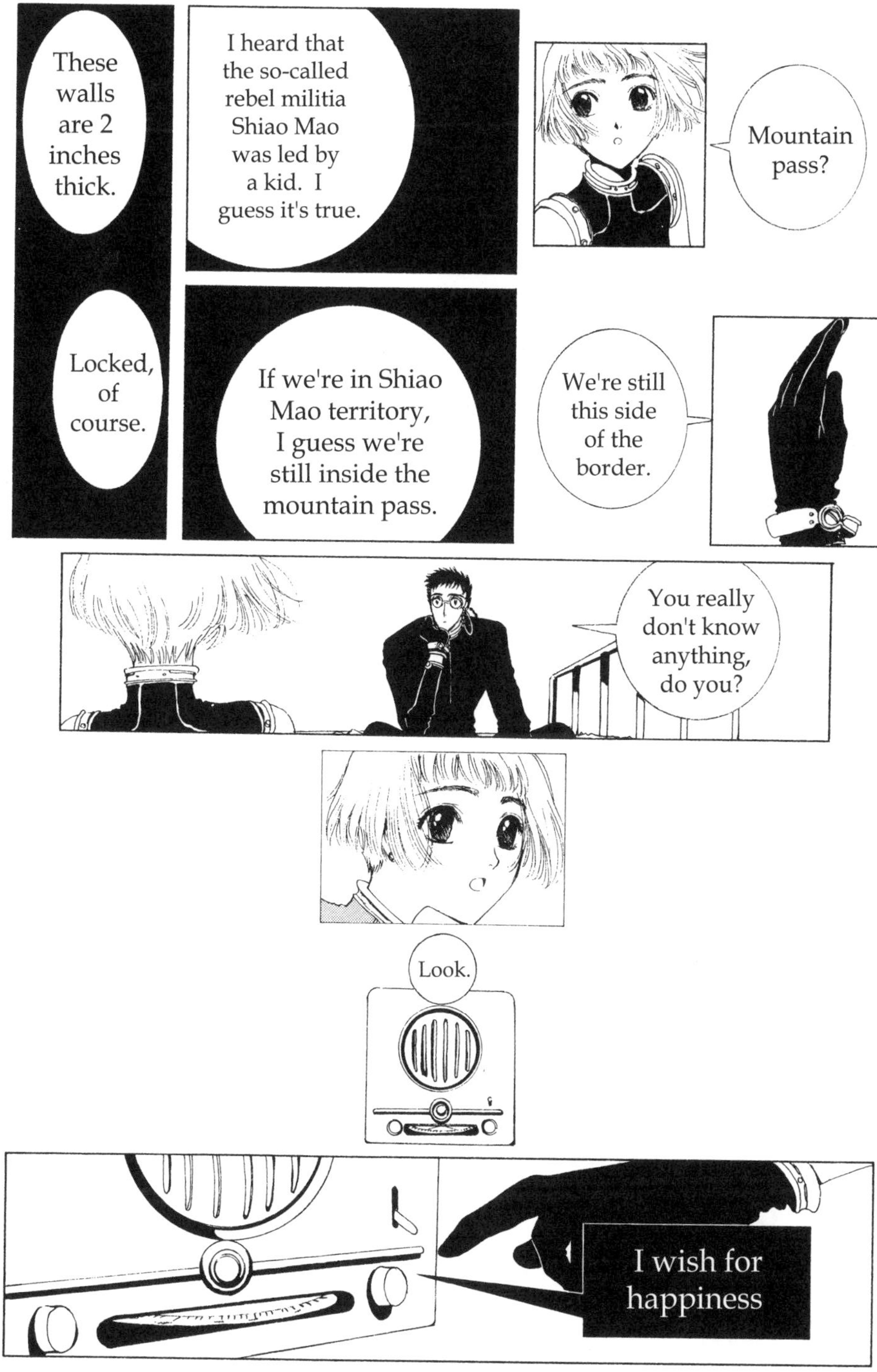
These walls are 2 inches thick.
Locked, of course.
I heard that the so-called rebel militia Shiao Mao was led by a kid. I guess it's true.
If we're in Shiao Mao territory, I guess we're still inside the mountain pass.
Mountain pass?
We're still this side of the border.
You really don't know anything, do you?
Look.
I wish for happiness

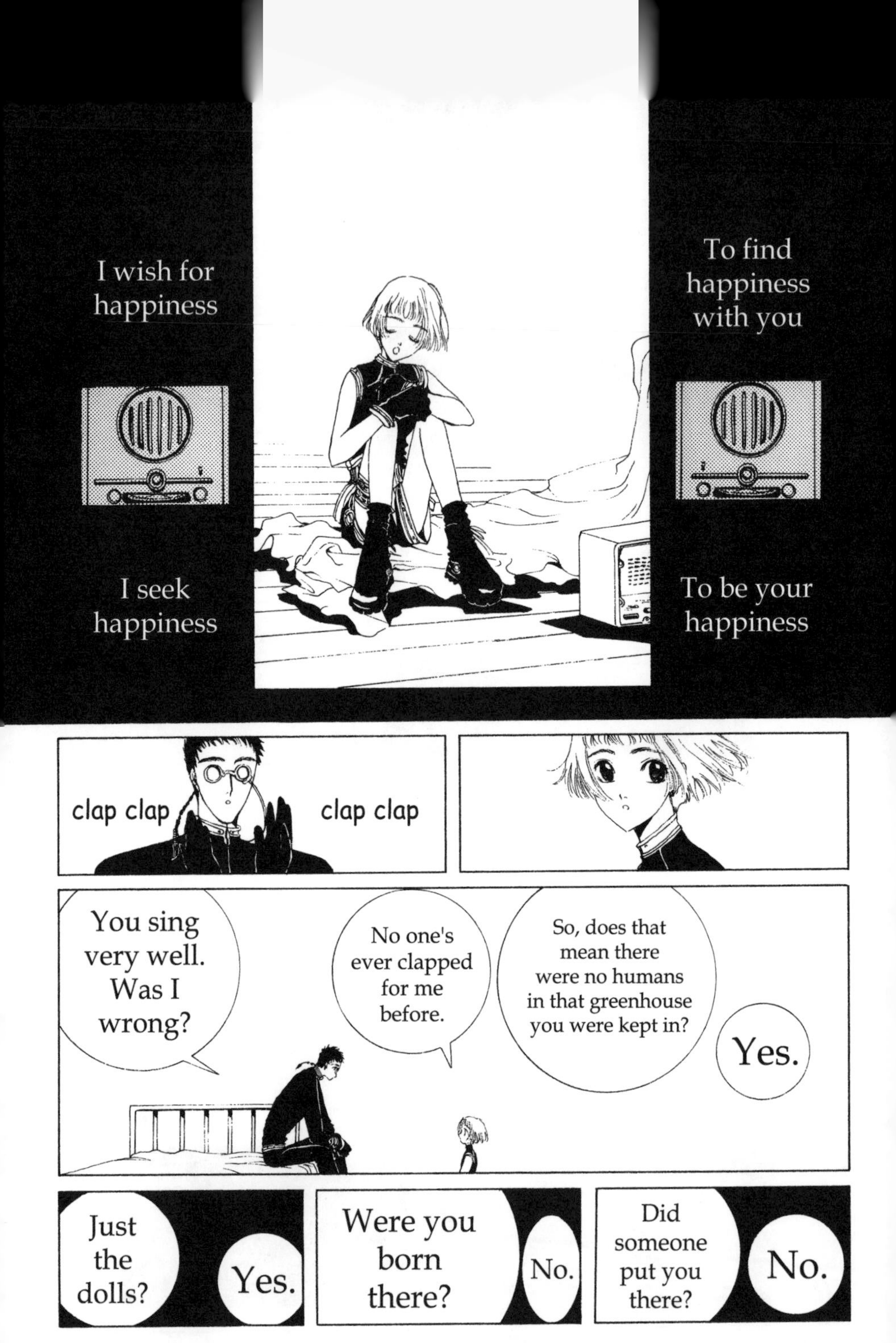
I wish for happiness
I seek happiness
To find happiness with you
To be your happiness
clap clap
clap clap
You sing very well. Was I wrong?
No one's ever clapped for me before.
So, does that mean there were no humans in that greenhouse you were kept in?
Yes.
Just the dolls?
Yes.
Were you born there?
No.
Did someone put you there?
No.

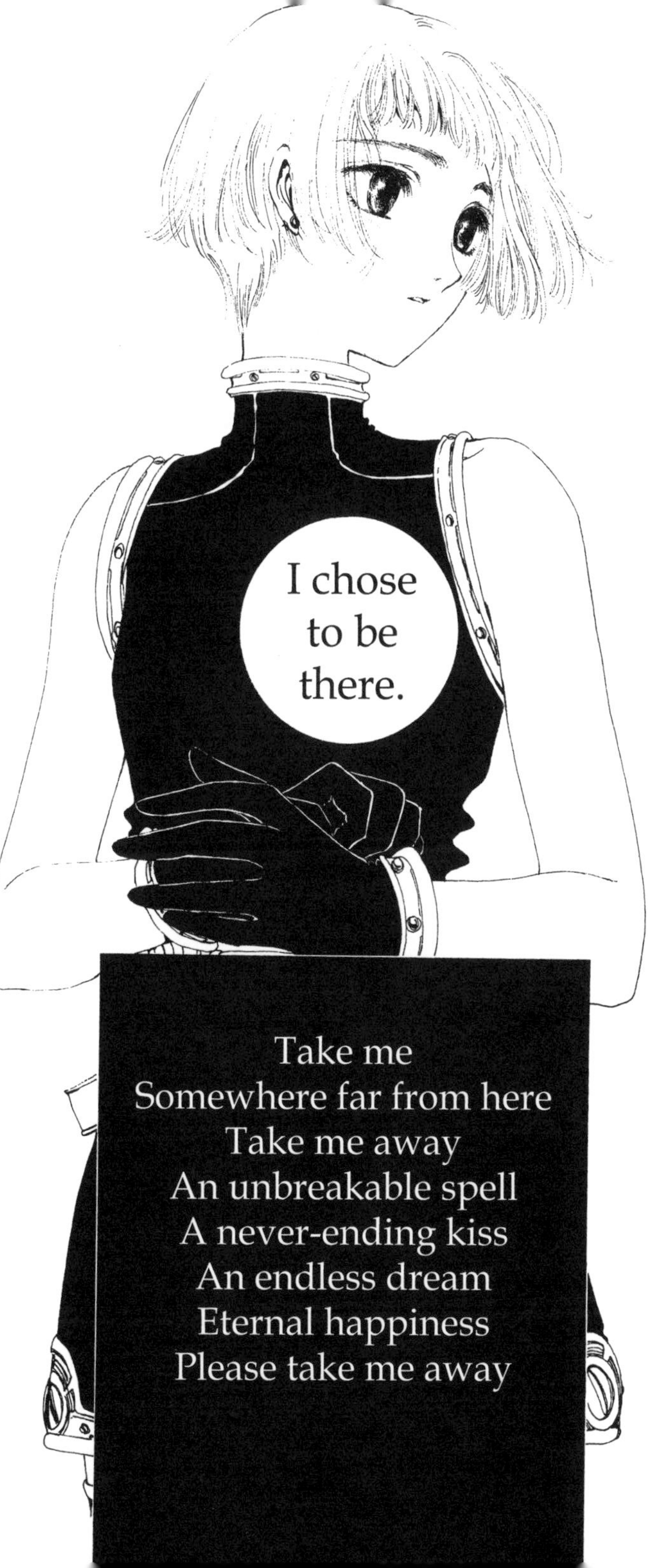
I chose to be there.
Take me
Somewhere far from here
Take me away
An unbreakable spell
A never-ending kiss
An endless dream
Eternal happiness
Please take me away

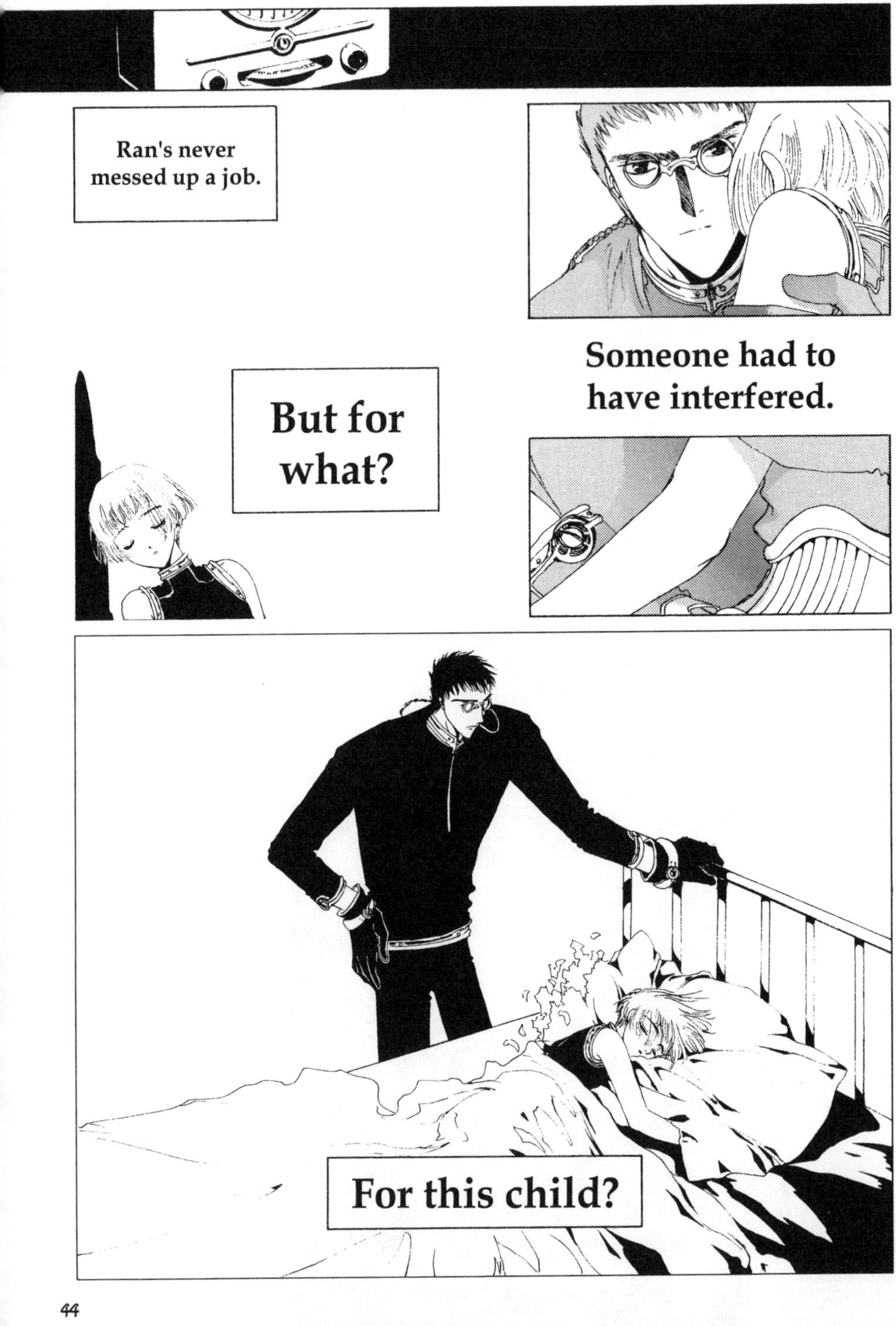
Ran's never messed up a job.
Someone had to have interfered.
But for what?
For this child?

Those soldiers
who attacked us…

They were Azaiean army.

So it's black
ops after all.
Another
General Ko
job, eh?

So now
I'm in
Azaiea.

Great.
Just
what
I need.

A TRACE

Looks like...

...you haven't changed a bit.

『跡』

But you know, Kazuhiko...

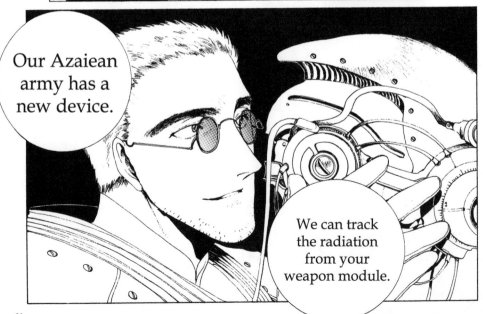

Our Azaiean army has a new device.

We can track the radiation from your weapon module.

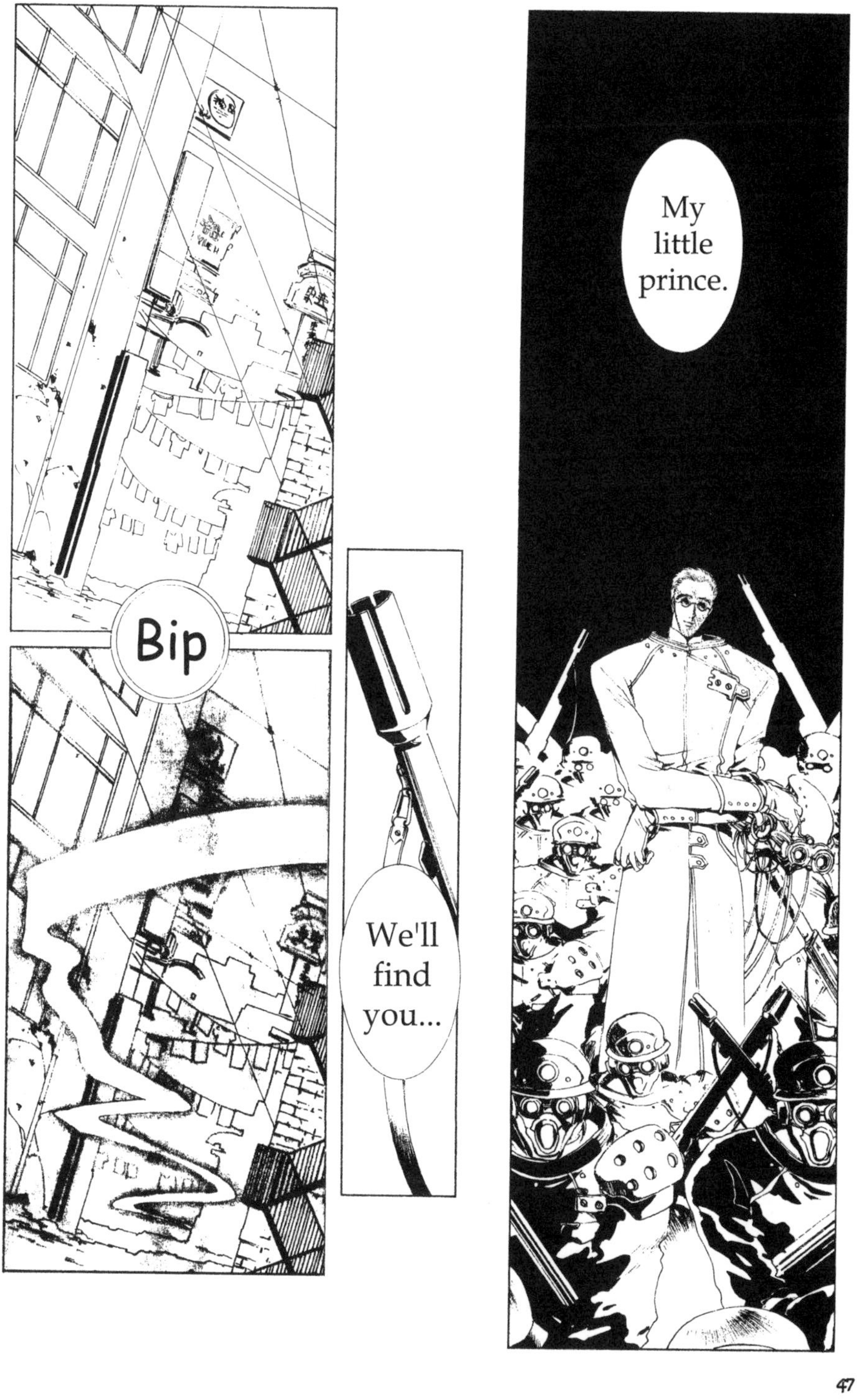
Bip
We'll find you...
My little prince.

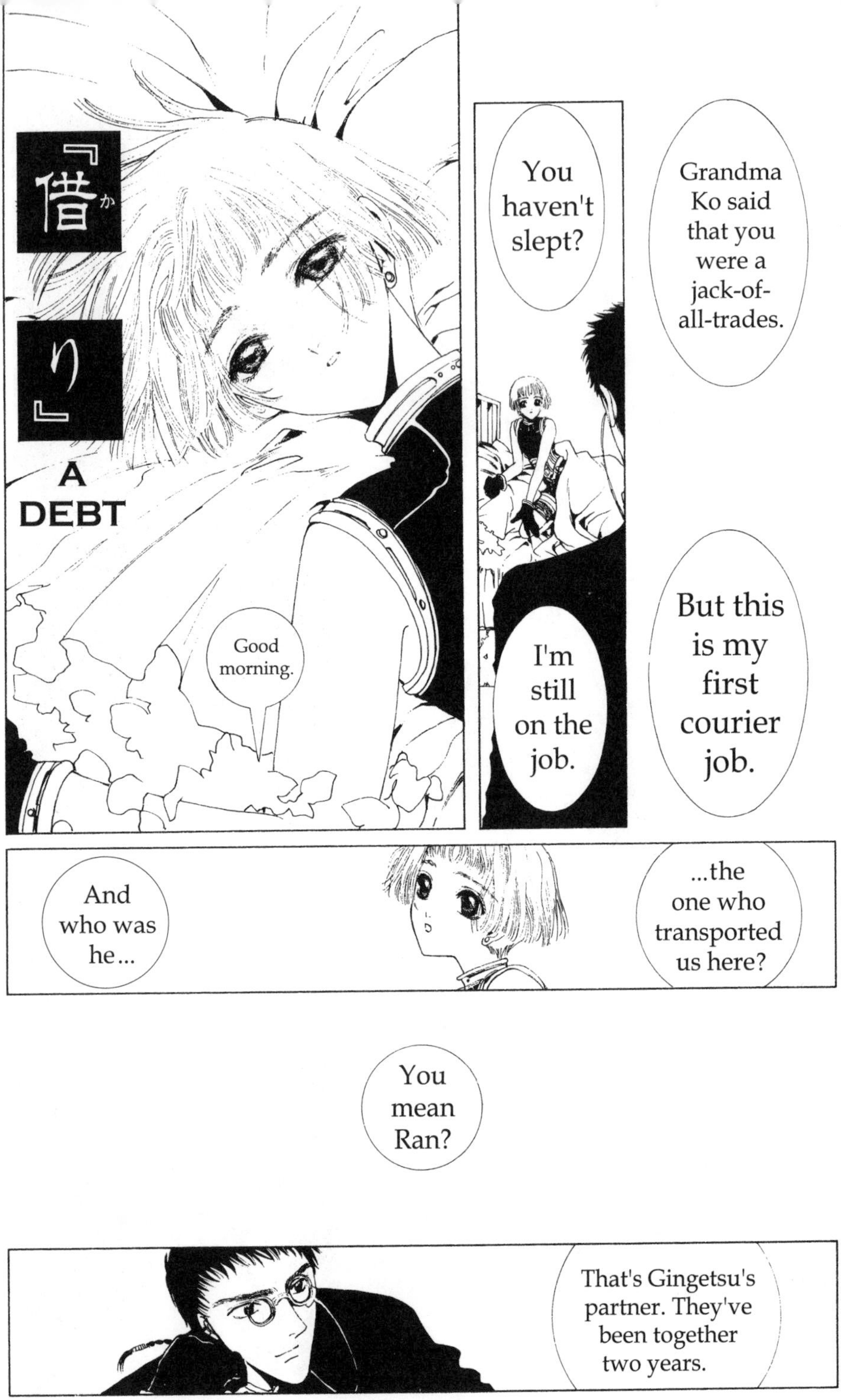
『借り』
A DEBT
Good morning.
You haven't slept?
Grandma Ko said that you were a jack-of-all-trades.
I'm still on the job.
But this is my first courier job.
And who was he...
...the one who transported us here?
You mean Ran?
That's Gingetsu's partner. They've been together two years.

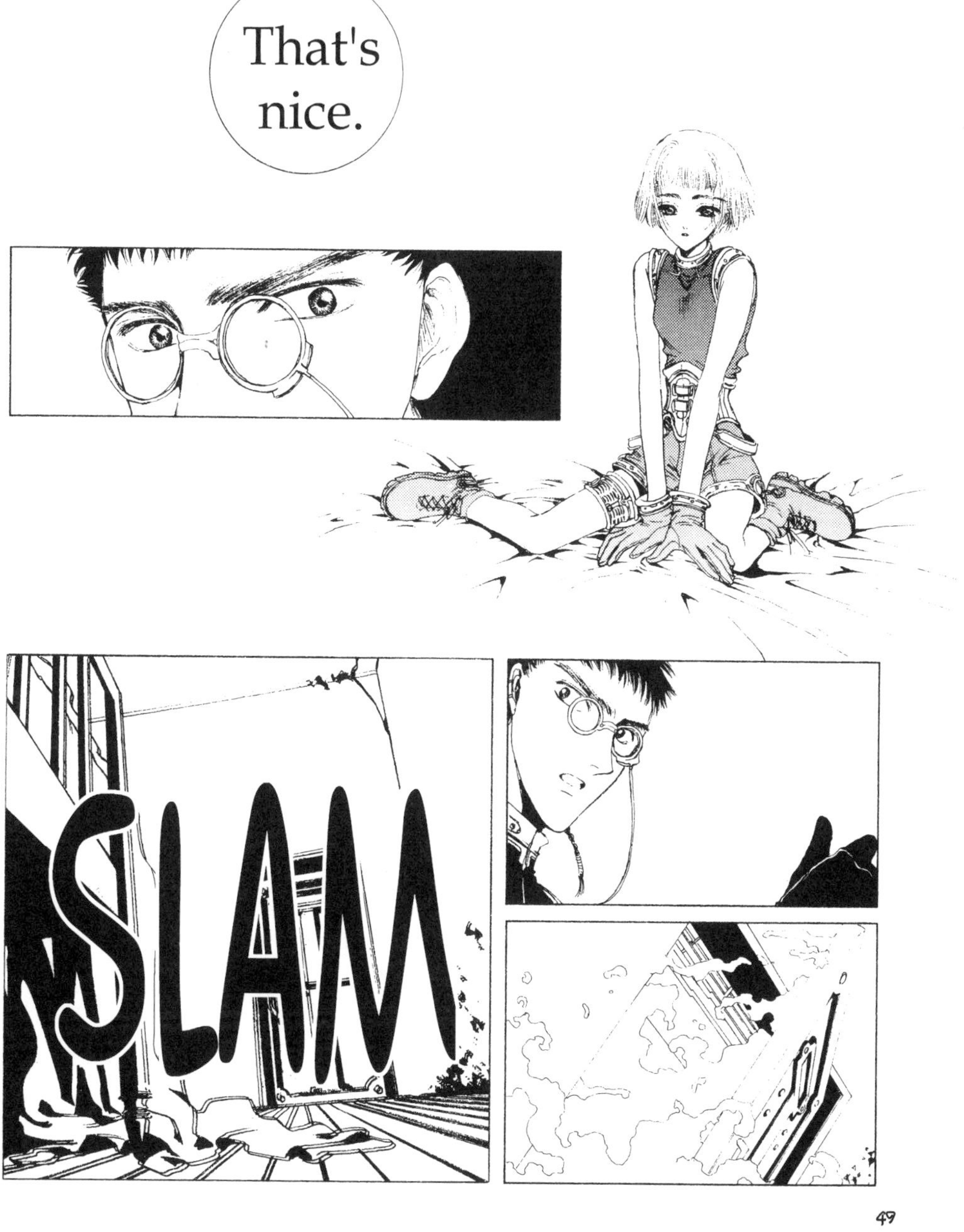
That's nice.
SLAM

We've uncovered your identity.

You're quick.

Creeek
Squeeek

Kazuhiko Fay Ryu. You're a famous man in the underground.

Your visitor told you that?

He's here to see you.

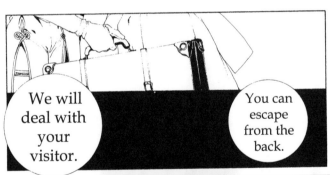

We will deal with your visitor.

You can escape from the back.

Why are you helping us?

When my soldiers surrounded you, why did you choose not to fight?

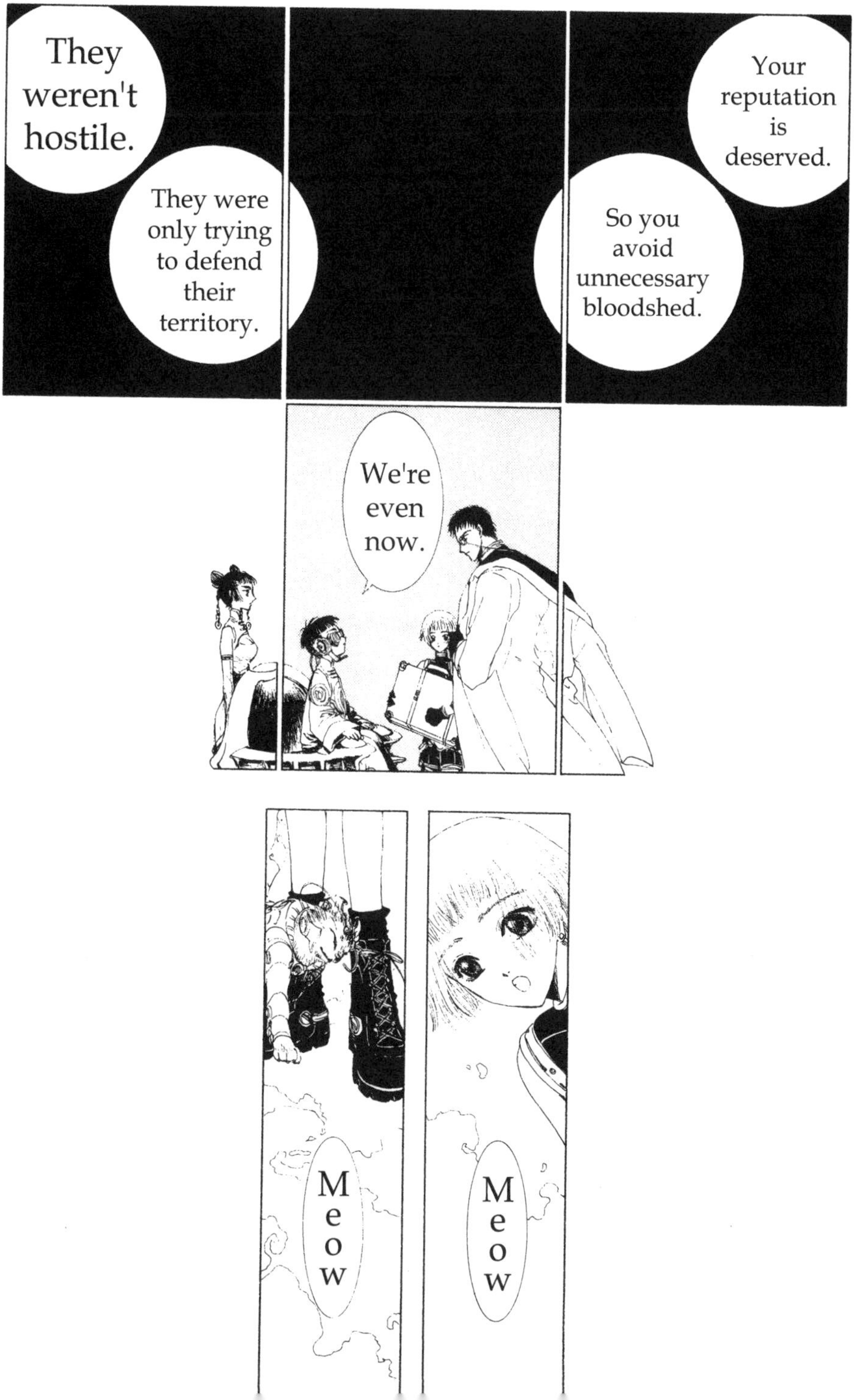
They weren't hostile.
They were only trying to defend their territory.
Your reputation is deserved.
So you avoid unnecessary bloodshed.
We're even now.
Meow
Meow

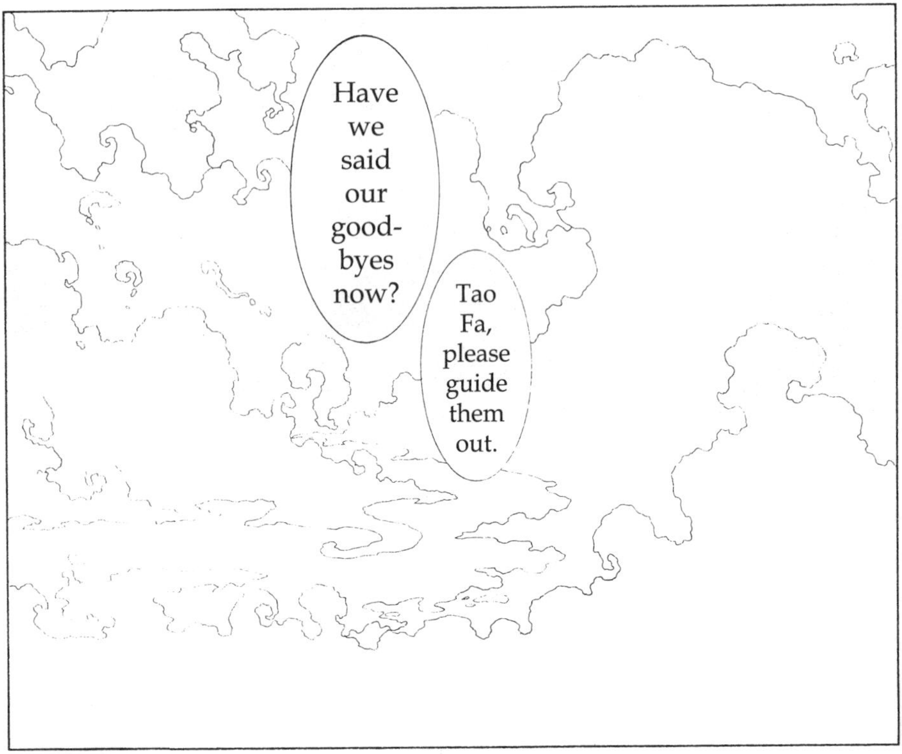
Have we said our good-byes now?
Tao Fa, please guide them out.

『花（はな）』 A FLOWER

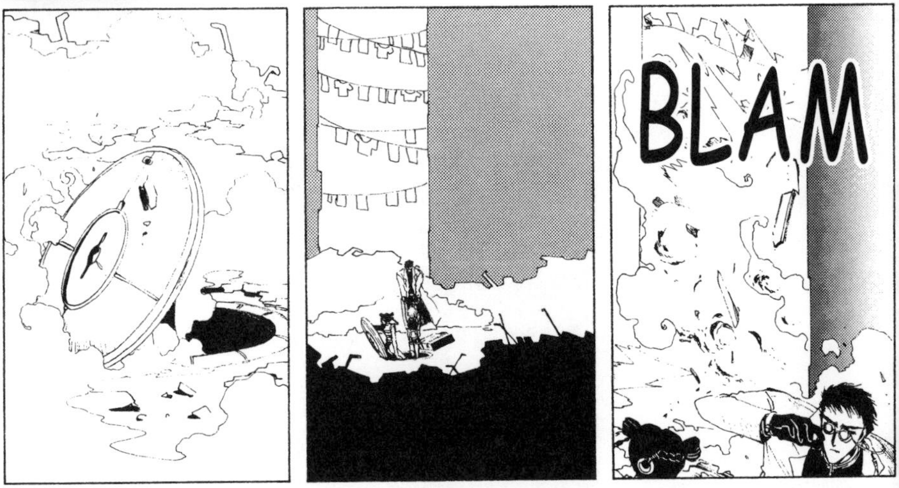
BLAM

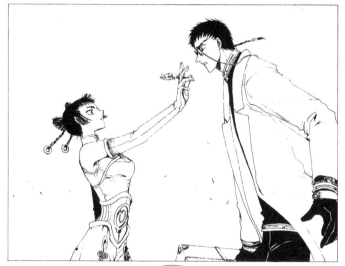

I hope you
enjoy the
rest of
your date.

BOOOOOM

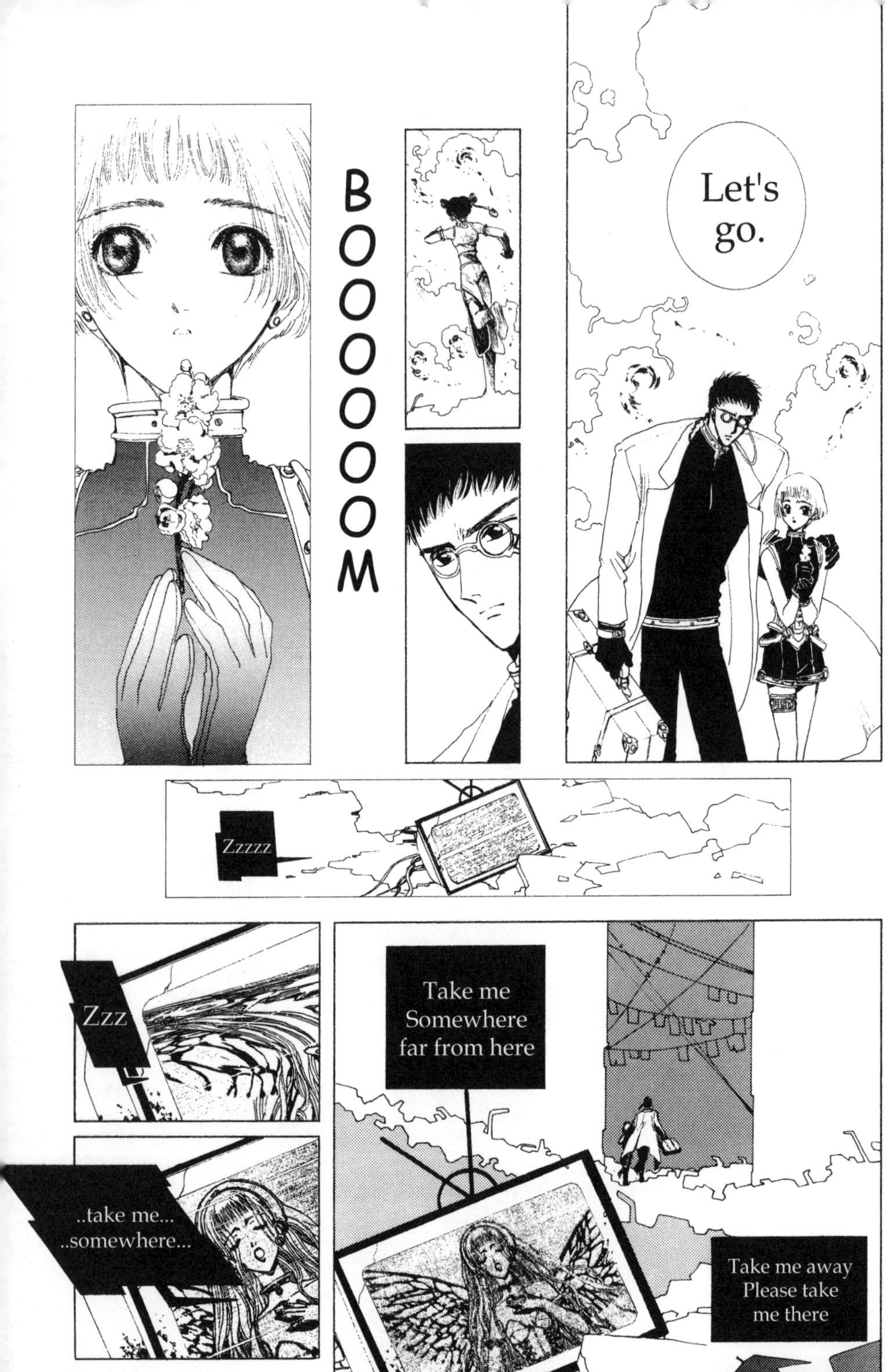
BOOOOOOM
Let's go.
Zzzzz
Zzz
..take me...
..somewhere...
Take me
Somewhere
far from here
Take me away
Please take
me there

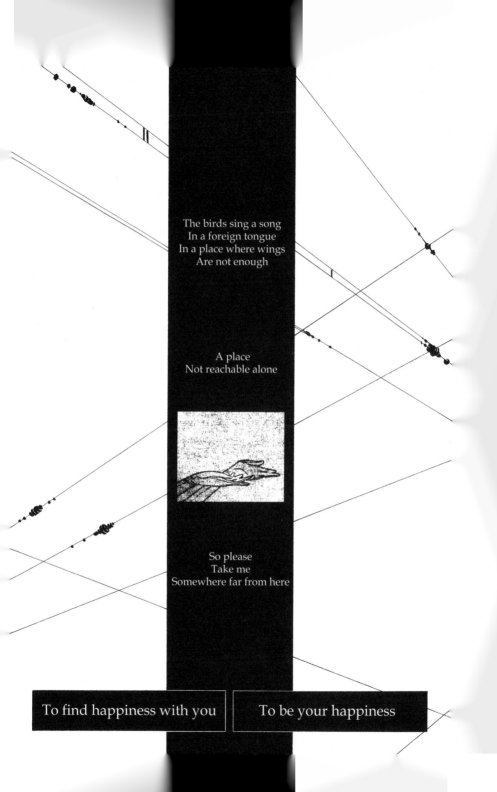

The birds sing a song
In a foreign tongue
In a place where wings
Are not enough

A place
Not reachable alone

So please
Take me
Somewhere far from here

To find happiness with you

To be your happiness

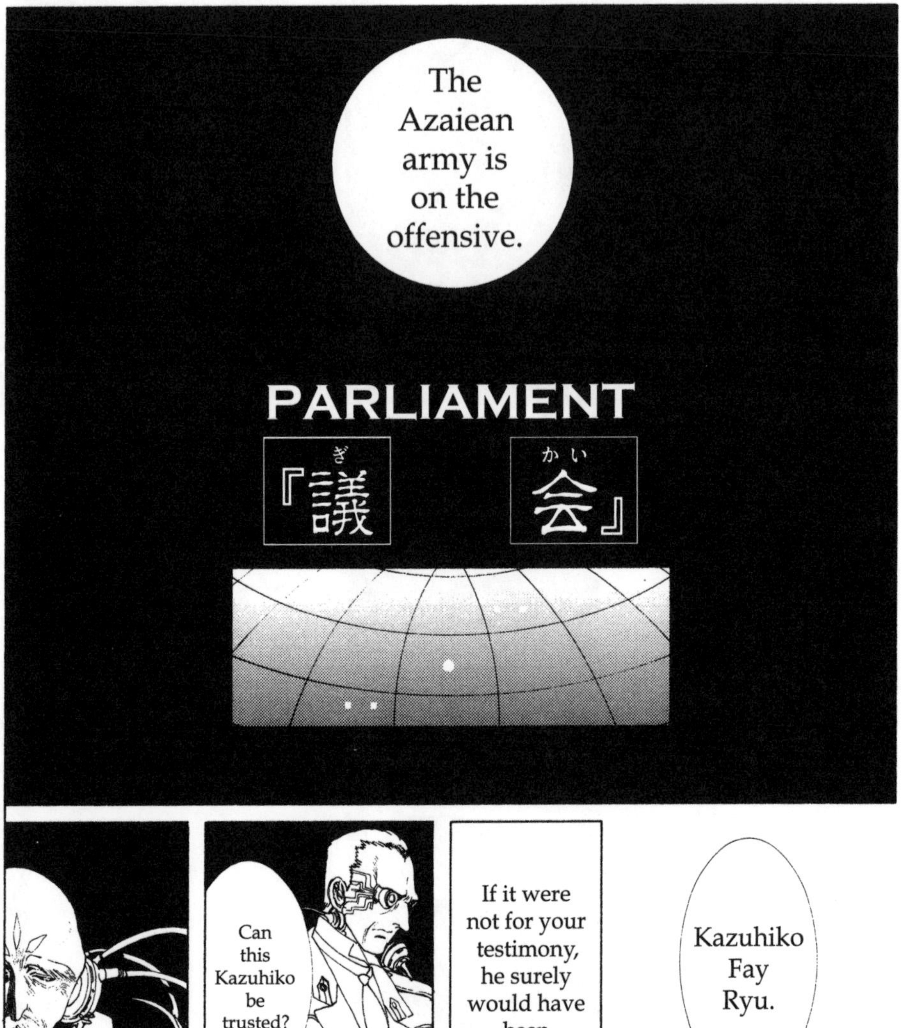
The Azaiean army is on the offensive.
PARLIAMENT
『議会』
No secret stays one for long. Especially one so precious.
Can this Kazuhiko be trusted?
He was a brilliant soldier, but he was also a trouble-maker.
If it were not for your testimony, he surely would have been imprisoned.
Kazuhiko Fay Ryu.
Former Secret Operations Deputy Commander.

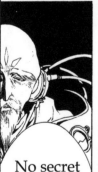

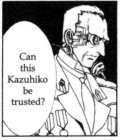

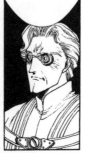

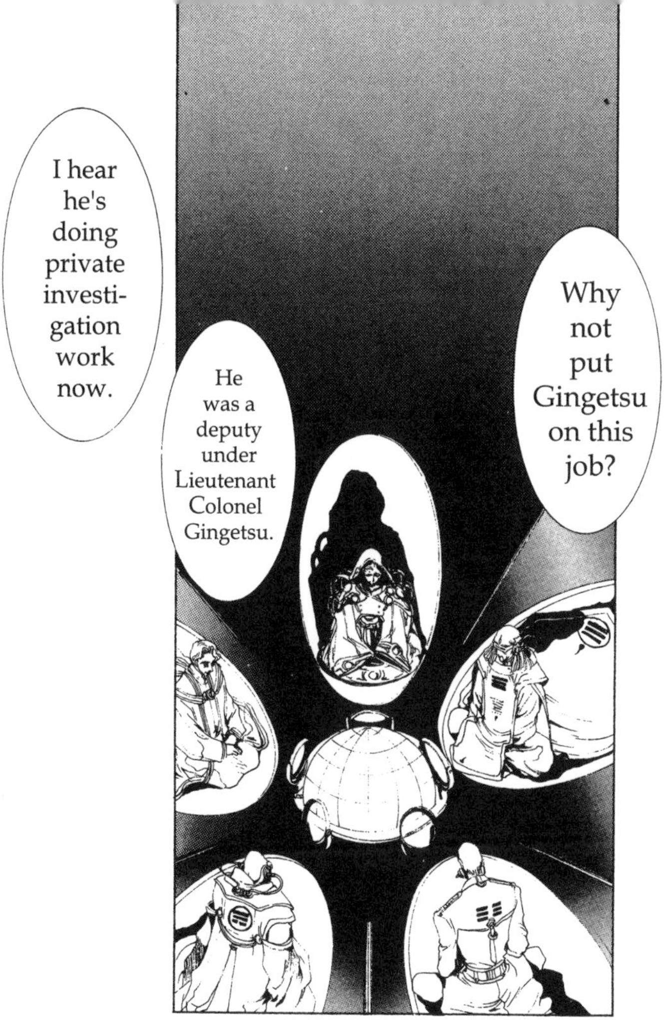
I hear he's doing private investigation work now.
He was a deputy under Lieutenant Colonel Gingetsu.
Why not put Gingetsu on this job?

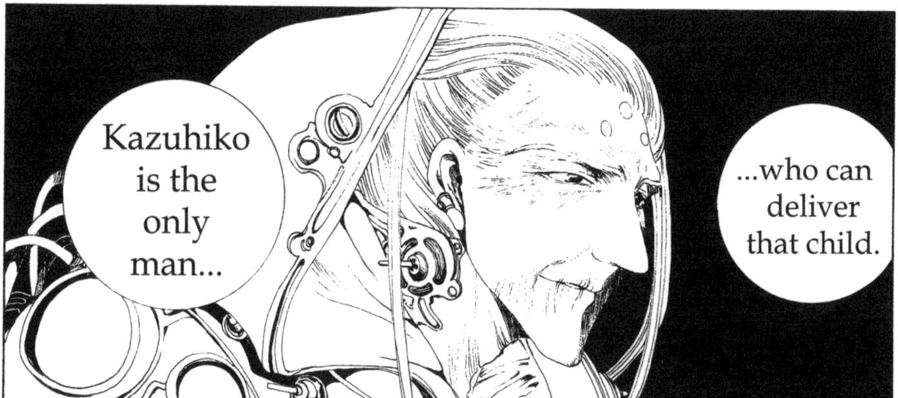
Kazuhiko is the only man...
...who can deliver that child.

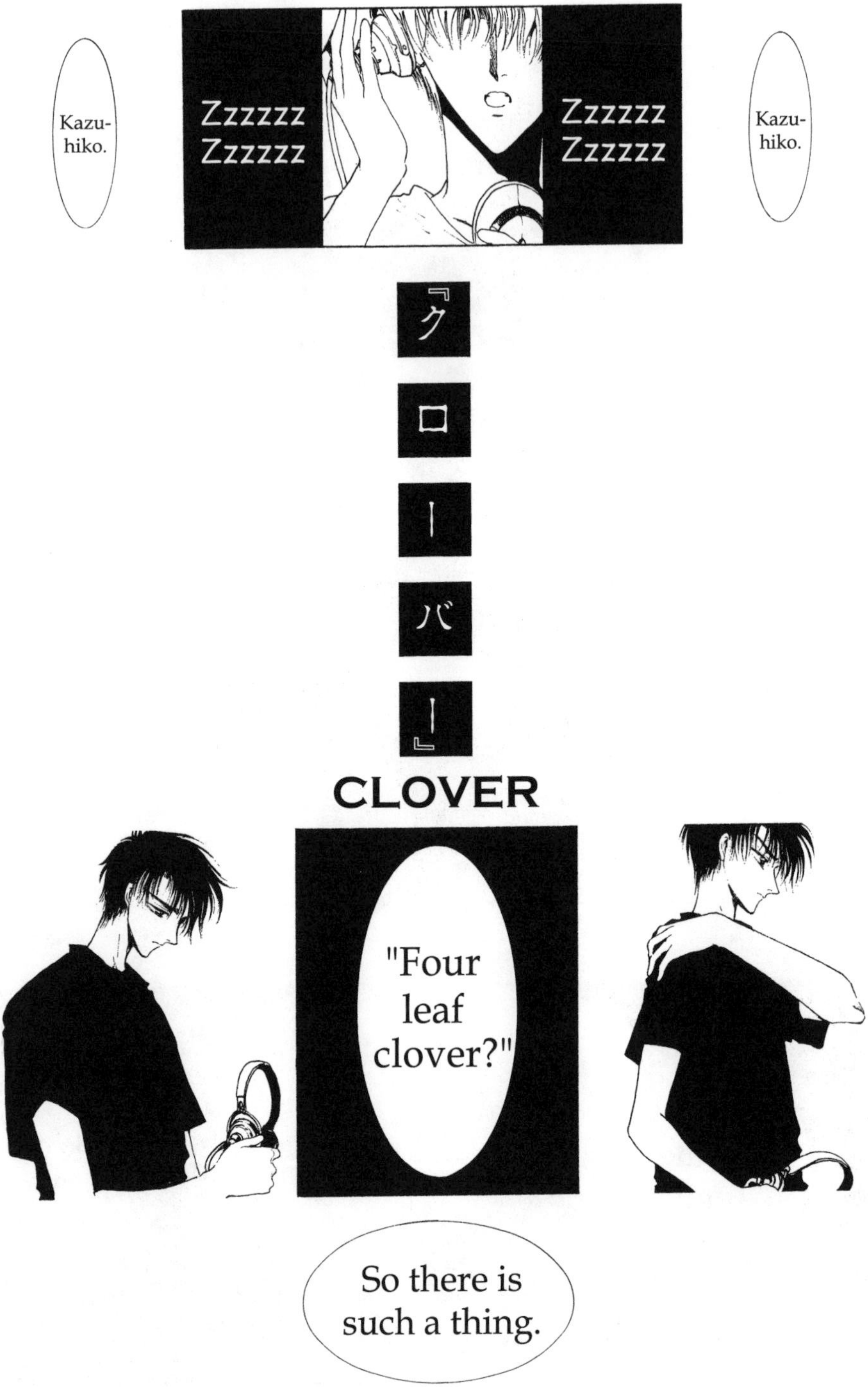
Kazu-hiko.
Zzzzzz Zzzzzz
Zzzzzz Zzzzzz
Kazu-hiko.
『クローバー』
CLOVER
"Four leaf clover?"
So there is such a thing.

『電話』
A TELEPHONE

Zzzzzz
Zzzzzz
Zzzzzz
Zzzzzz

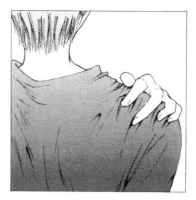

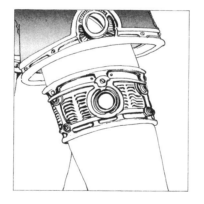

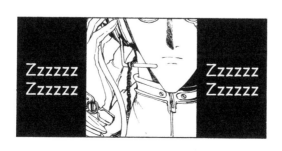

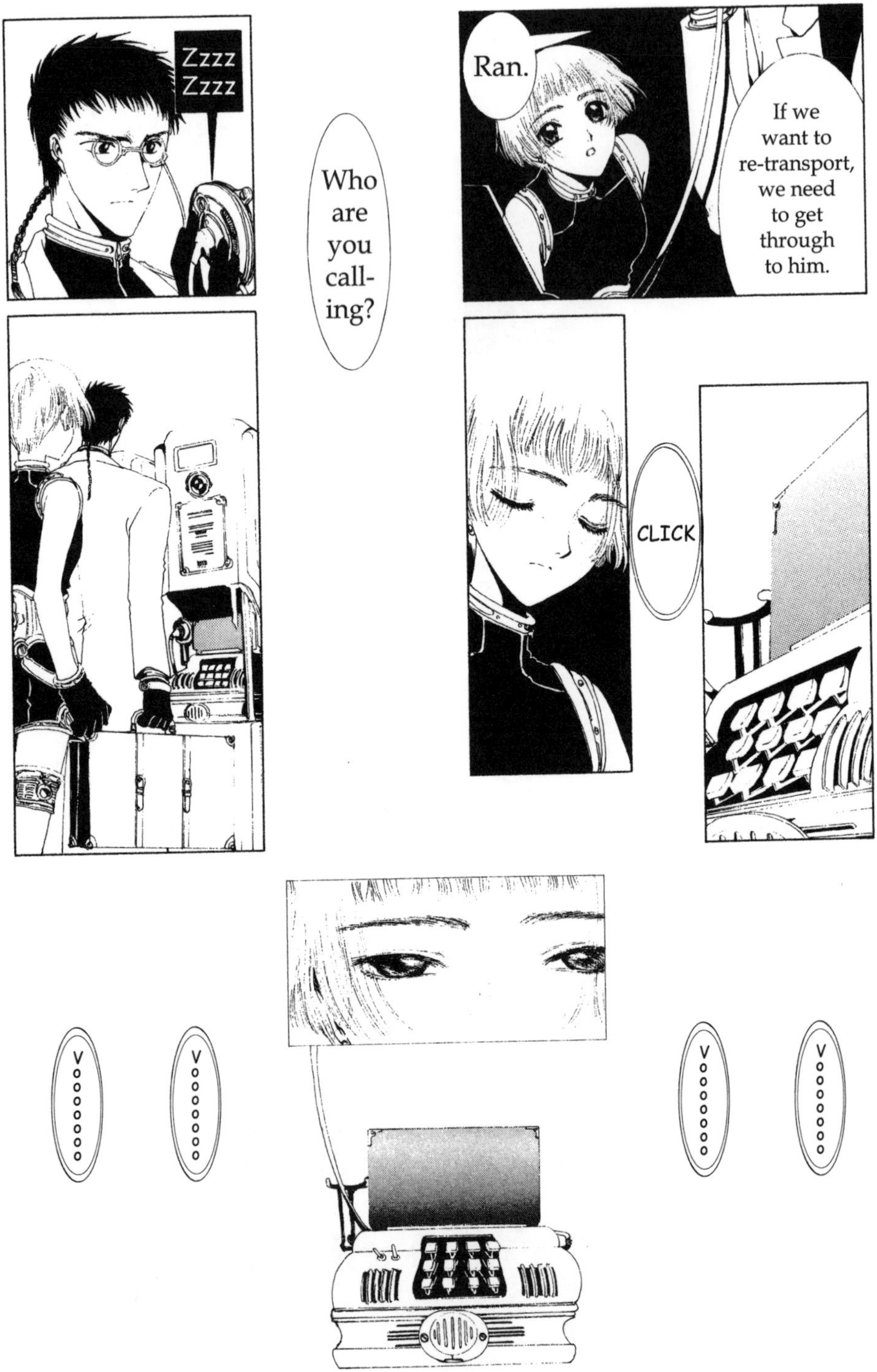
Zzzz Zzzz
Who are you call- ing?
Ran.
If we want to re-transport, we need to get through to him.
CLICK
Voooooooo
Voooooooo
Voooooooo
Voooooooo

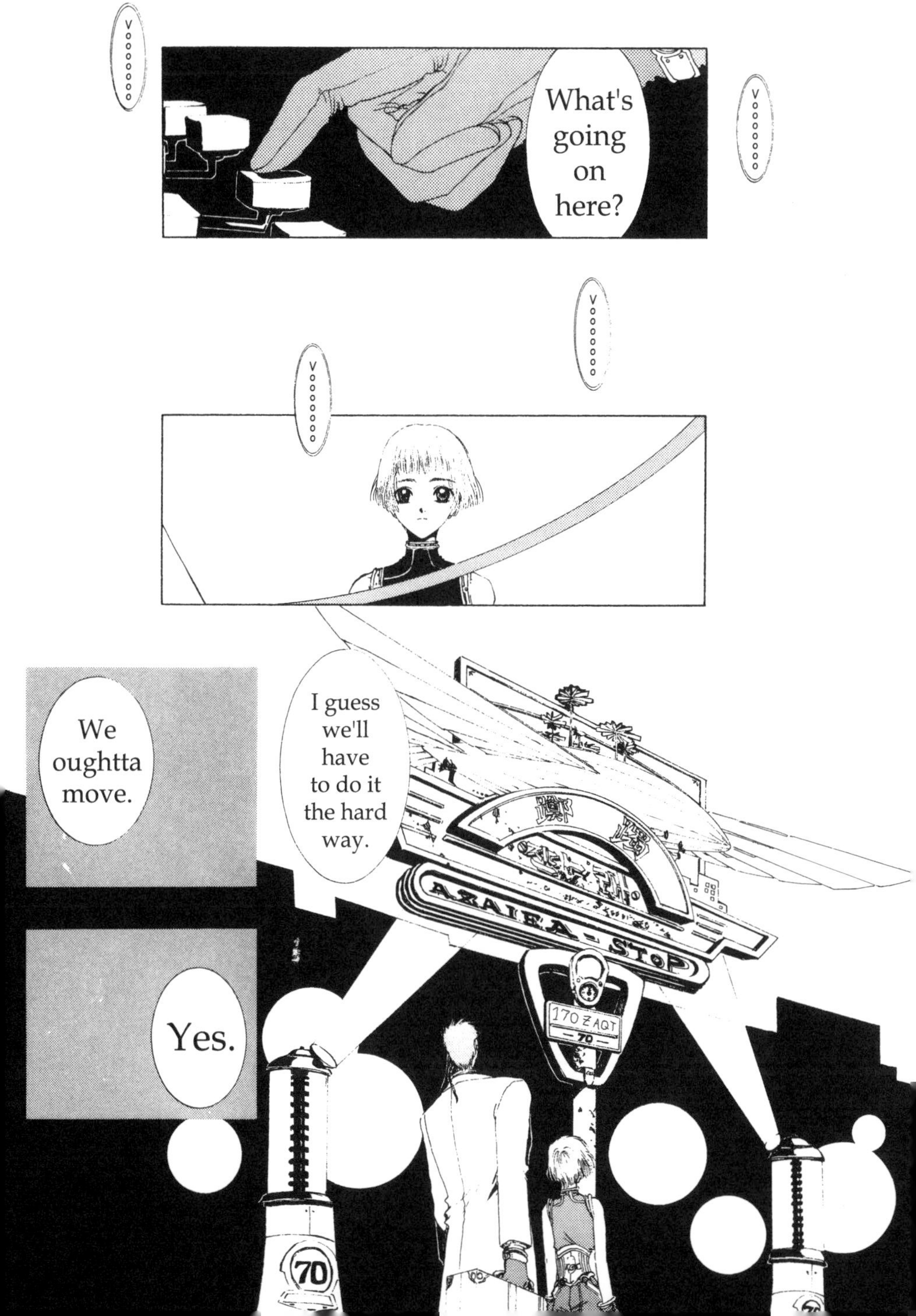
Vooooooo
What's going on here?
Vooooooo
Vooooooo
Vooooooo
We oughtta move.
I guess we'll have to do it the hard way.
Yes.
170 Z AQT
70
70

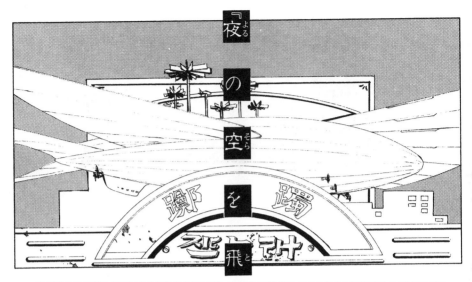

『夜の空を飛ぶ羽のはえた魚』

WINGED FISH THAT FLIES THROUGH THE NIGHT

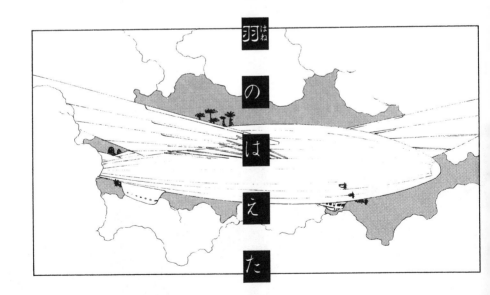

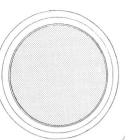

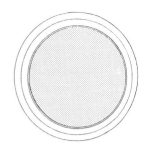

Your first time riding on one of these?

Yes.

CLICK

I wish for happiness

I seek happiness

To find happiness with you

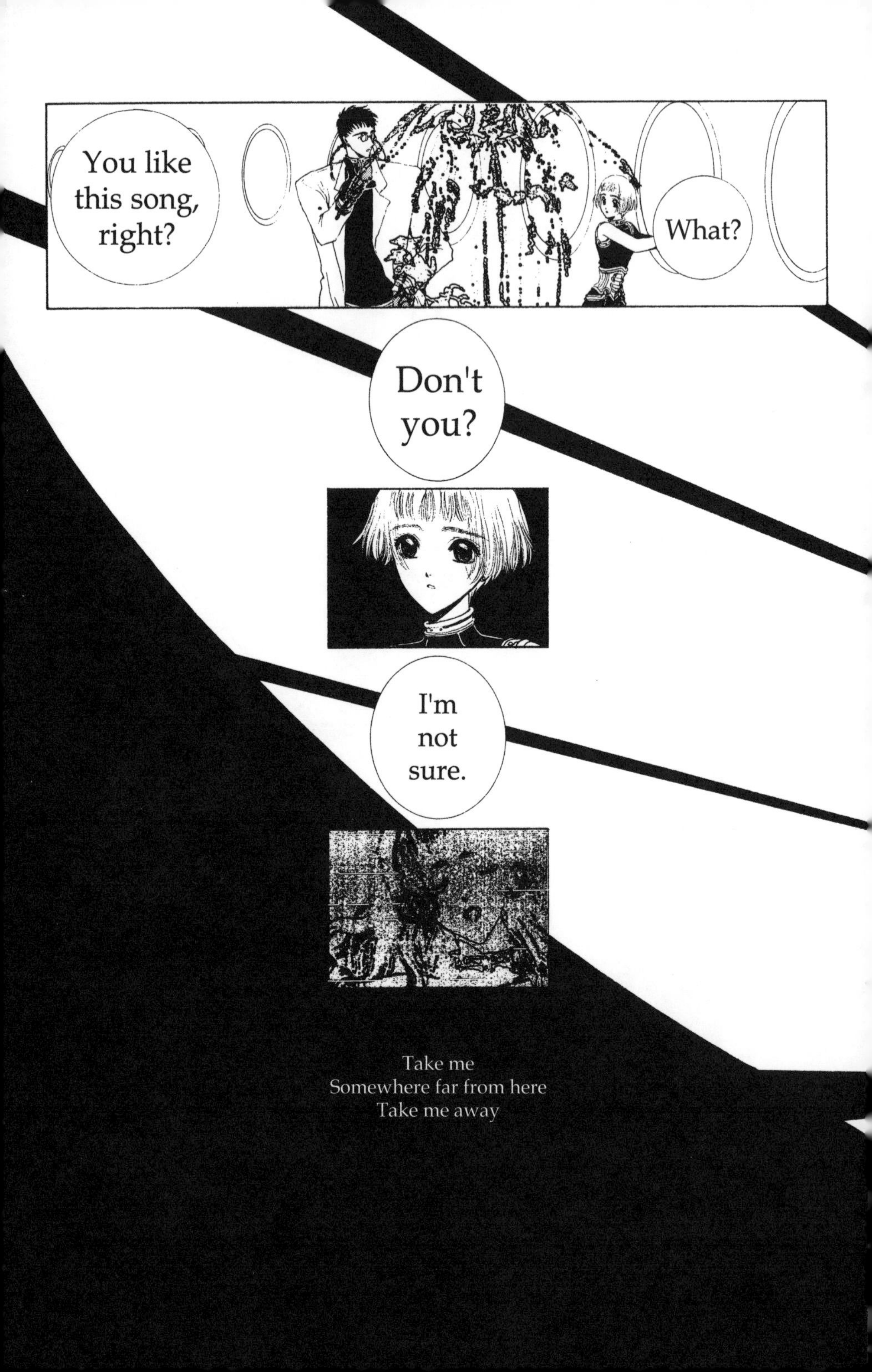
You like this song, right?
What?
Don't you?
I'm not sure.
Take me
Somewhere far from here
Take me away

The birds sing a song
In a foreign tongue
In a place where wings
Are not enough
A place
Not reachable alone

So please
Take me
Somewhere far from here

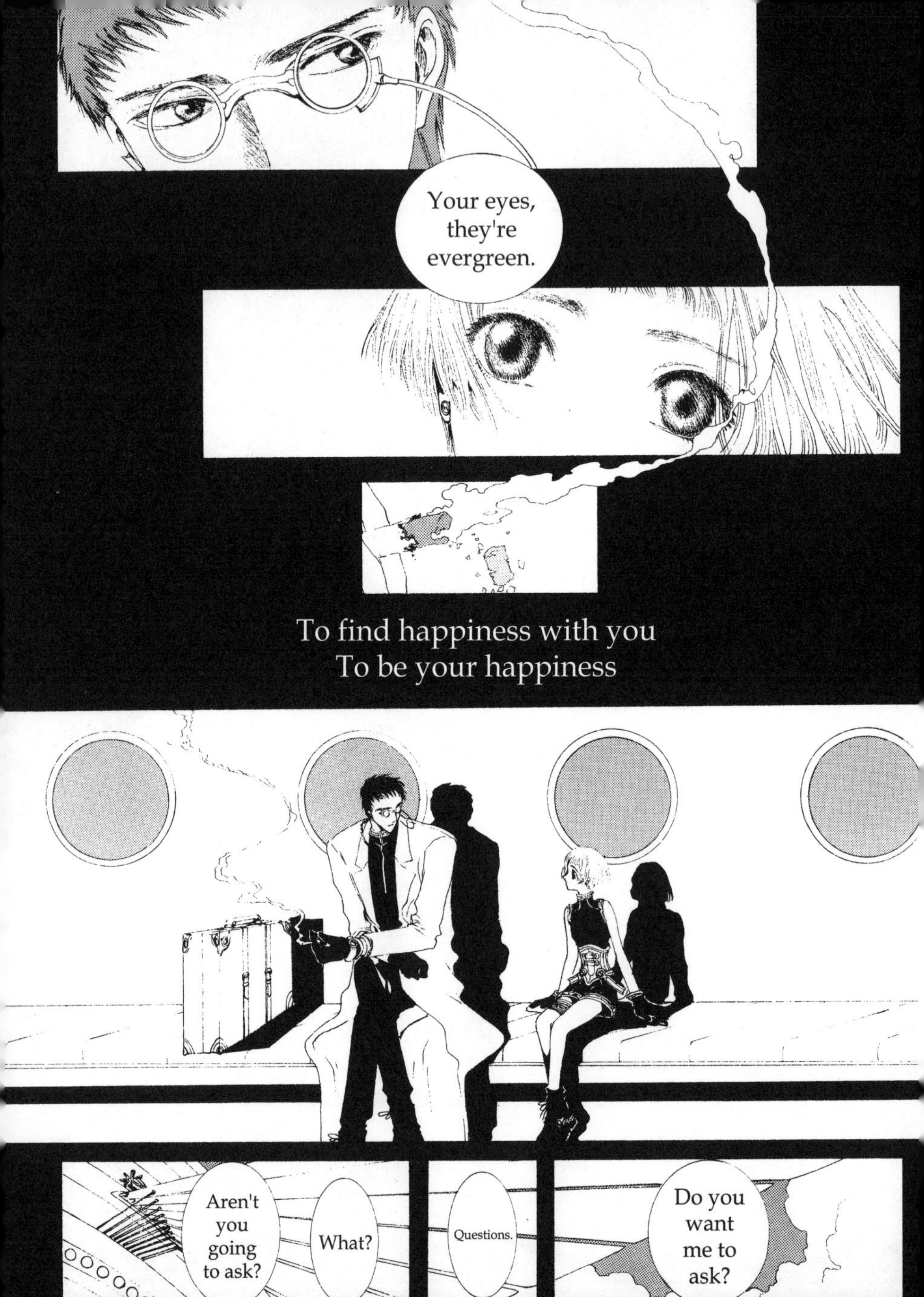
Your eyes, they're evergreen.
To find happiness with you
To be your happiness
Aren't you going to ask?
What?
Questions.
Do you want me to ask?

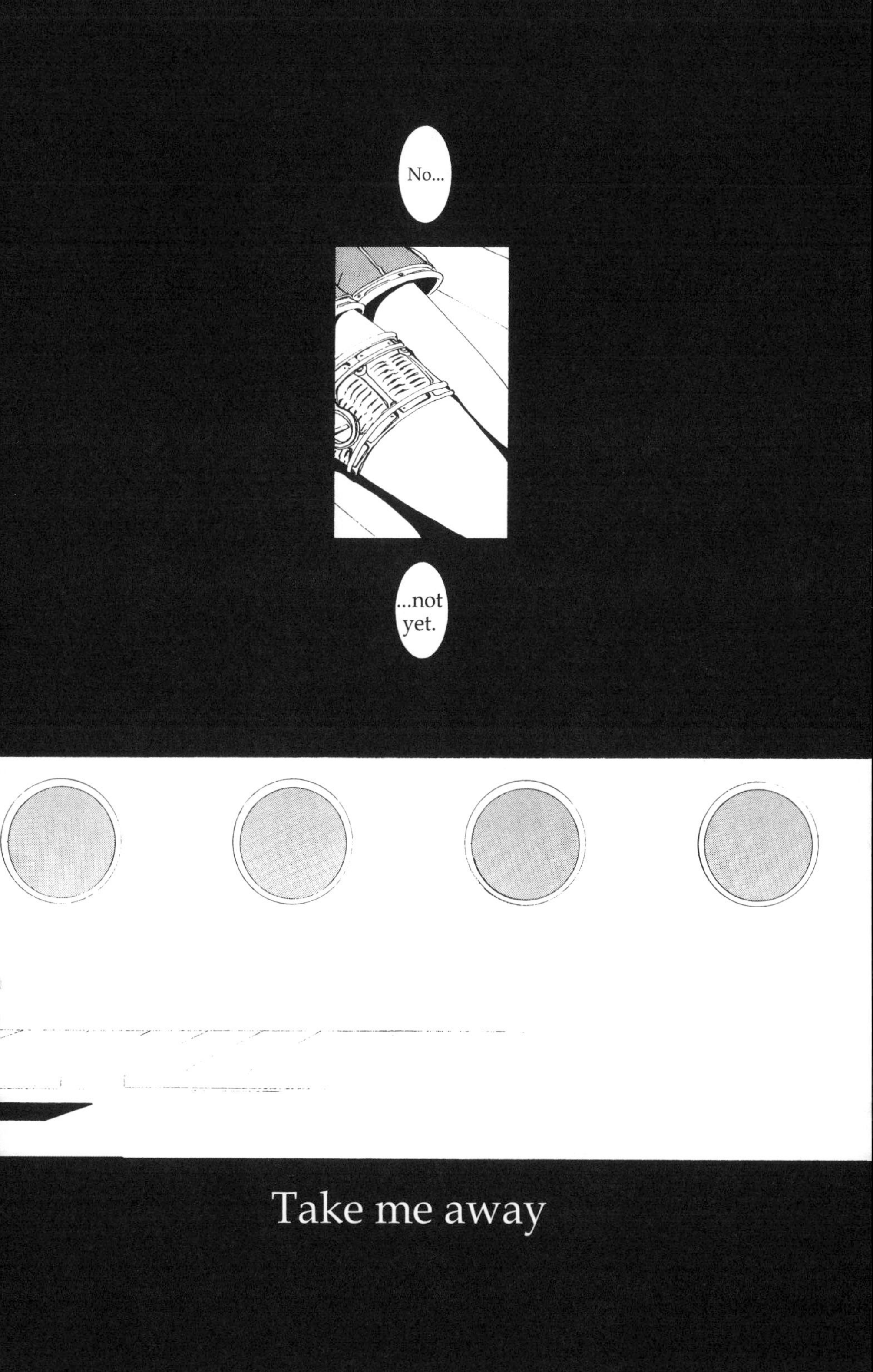
No...
...not yet.
Take me away

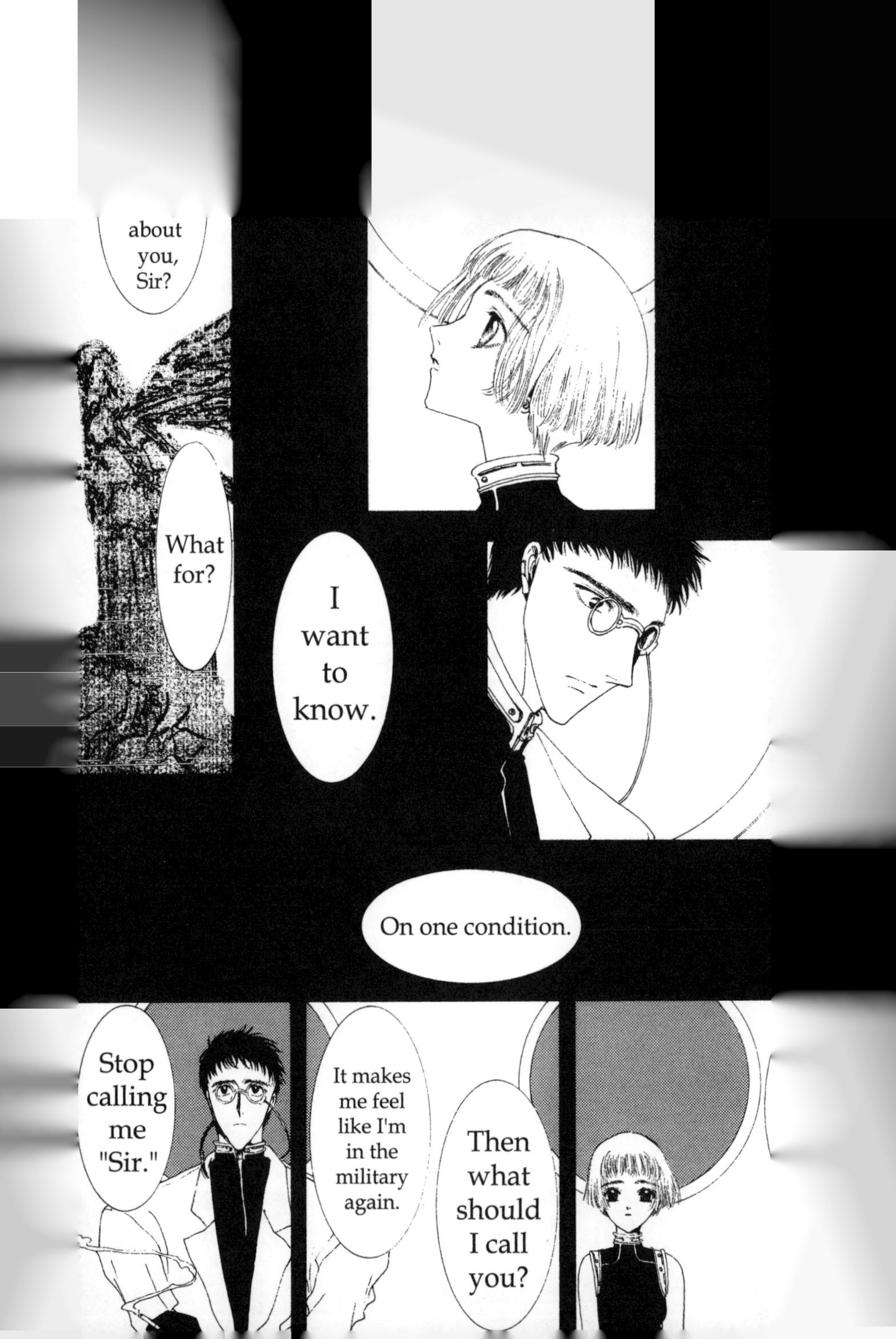
about you, Sir?
What for?
I want to know.
On one condition.
Stop calling me "Sir."
It makes me feel like I'm in the military again.
Then what should I call you?

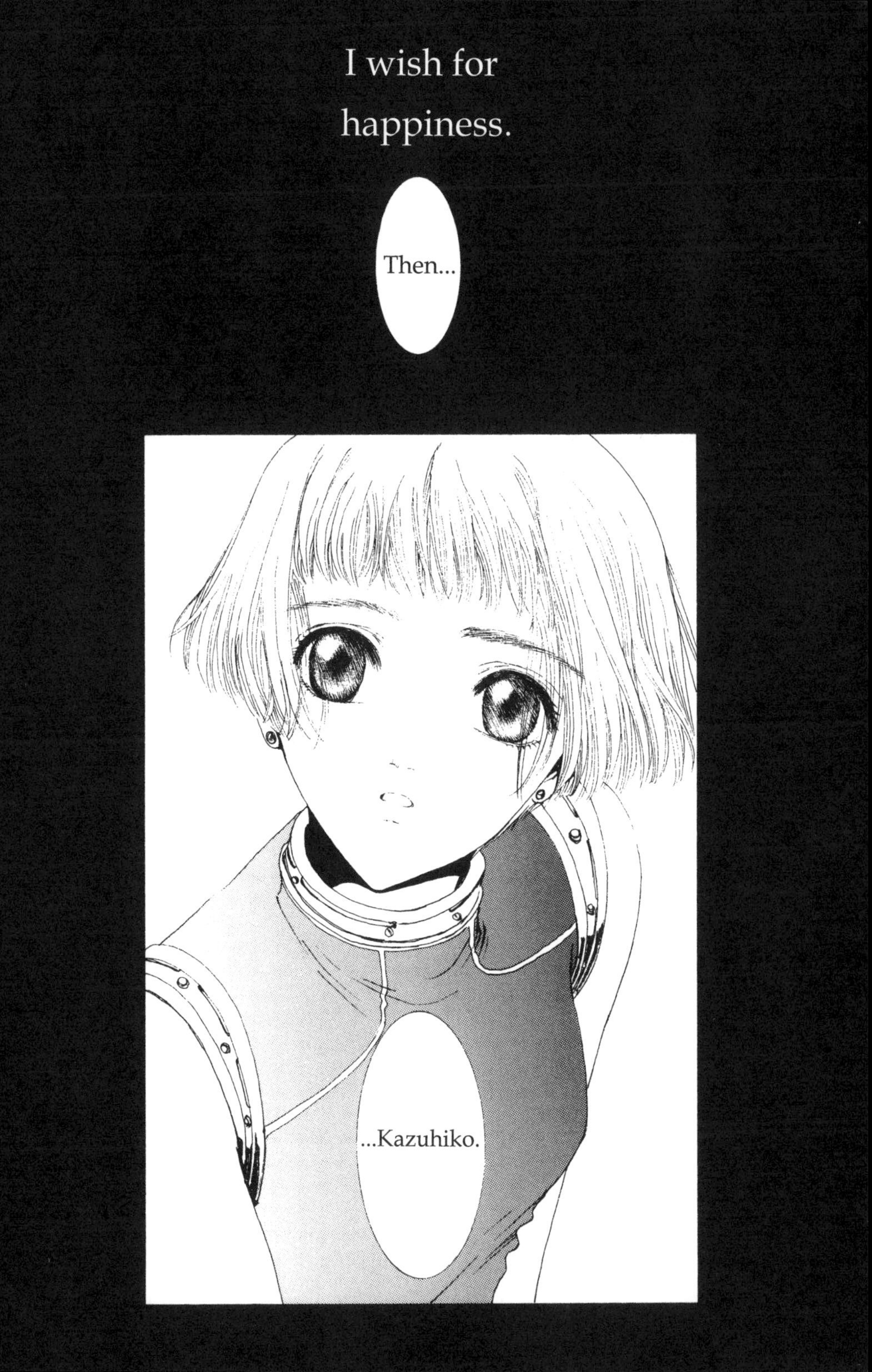
I wish for happiness.
Then...
...Kazuhiko.

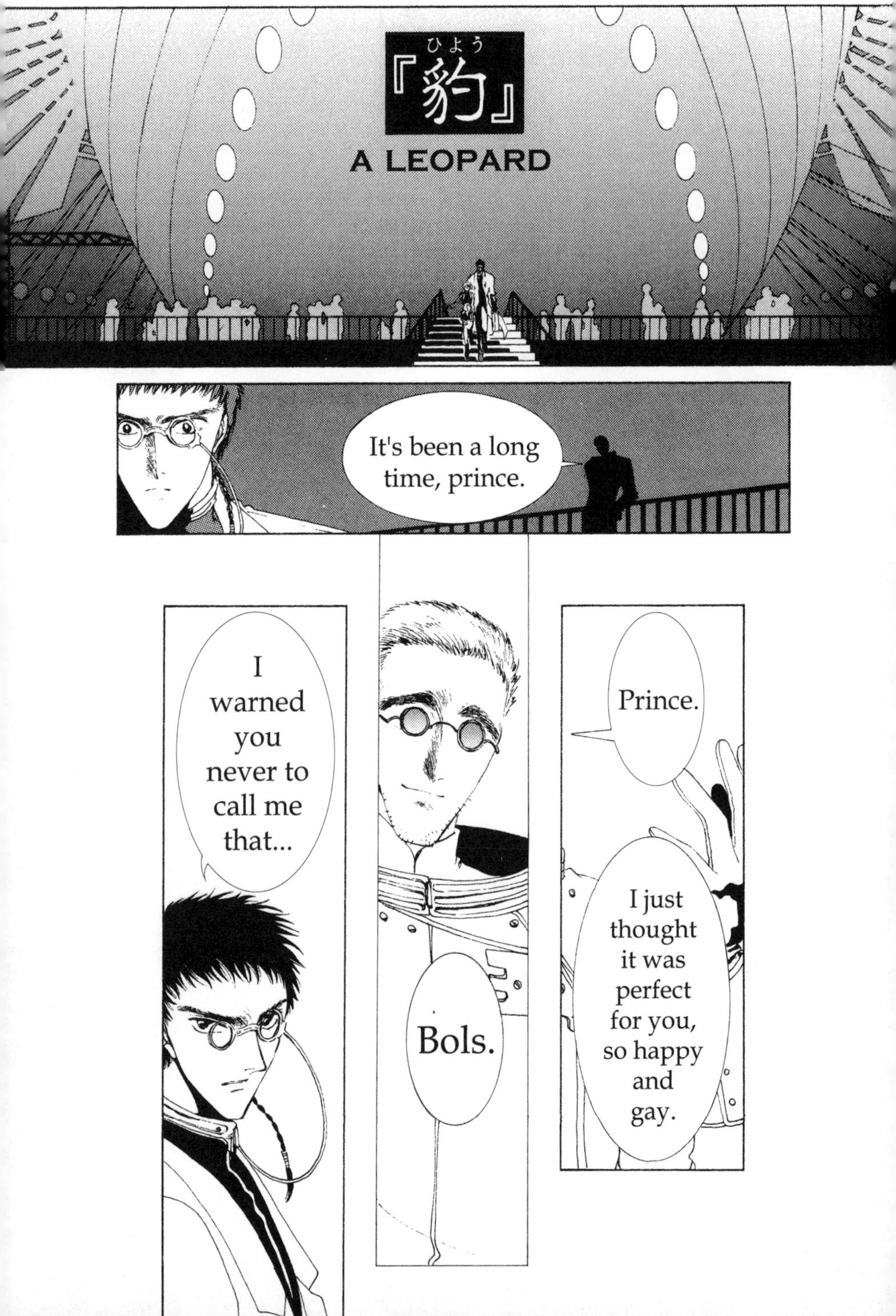
『豹』
ひょう
A LEOPARD
It's been a long time, prince.
I warned you never to call me that...
Bols.
Prince.
I just thought it was perfect for you, so happy and gay.

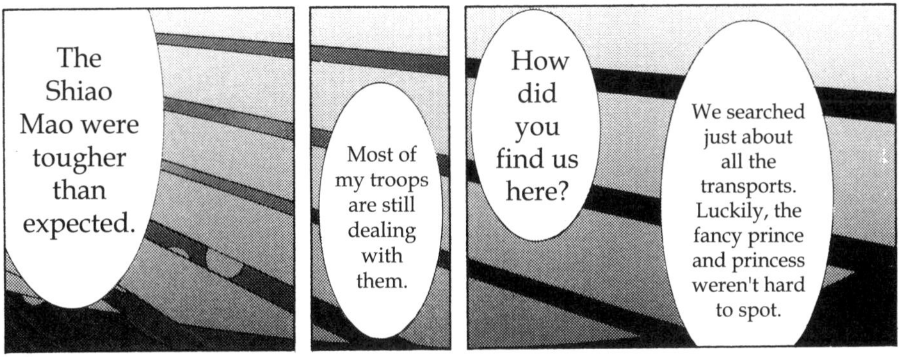
The Shiao Mao were tougher than expected.
Most of my troops are still dealing with them.
How did you find us here?
We searched just about all the transports. Luckily, the fancy prince and princess weren't hard to spot.

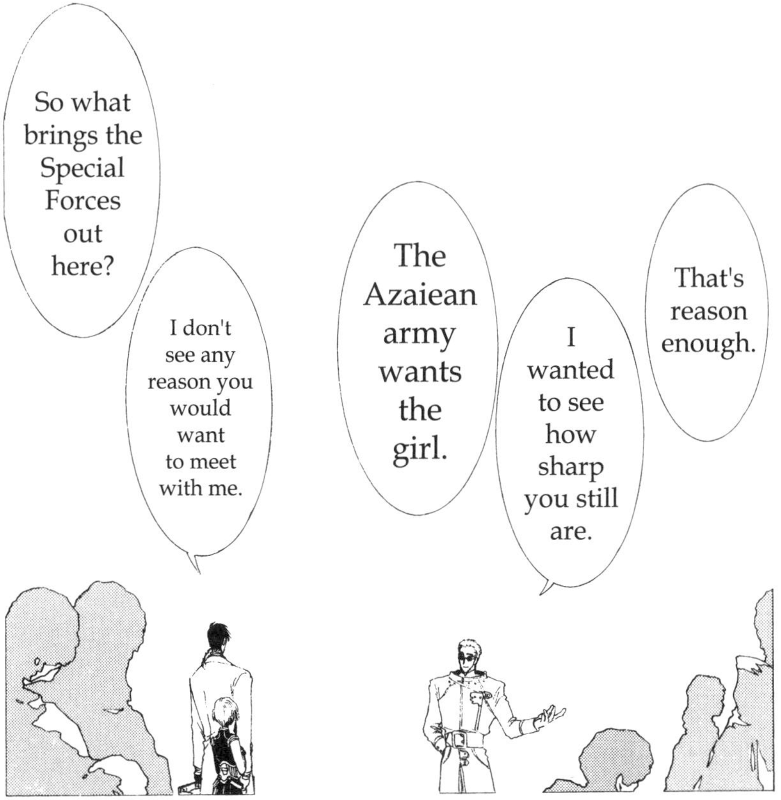
So what brings the Special Forces out here?
I don't see any reason you would want to meet with me.
The Azaiean army wants the girl.
I wanted to see how sharp you still are.
That's reason enough.

This
girl
is my
respon-
sibility.

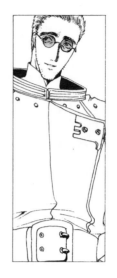

You
mean
the
Wizards?

I'm sure the
old buzzards of
the parliamentary
council would be
thrilled to hear
you call them
the Wizards.

I hear the
old farts control
most of the
underground
these days.

So anyway, if you're itching to go one-on-one, I'm ready.

What, here?

Don't be an idiot. We'll find an alleyway.

I don't mind if it's here.

I mind.

Don't wanna hurt innocent people?

That's the prince...

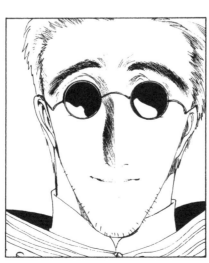

...I know and love.

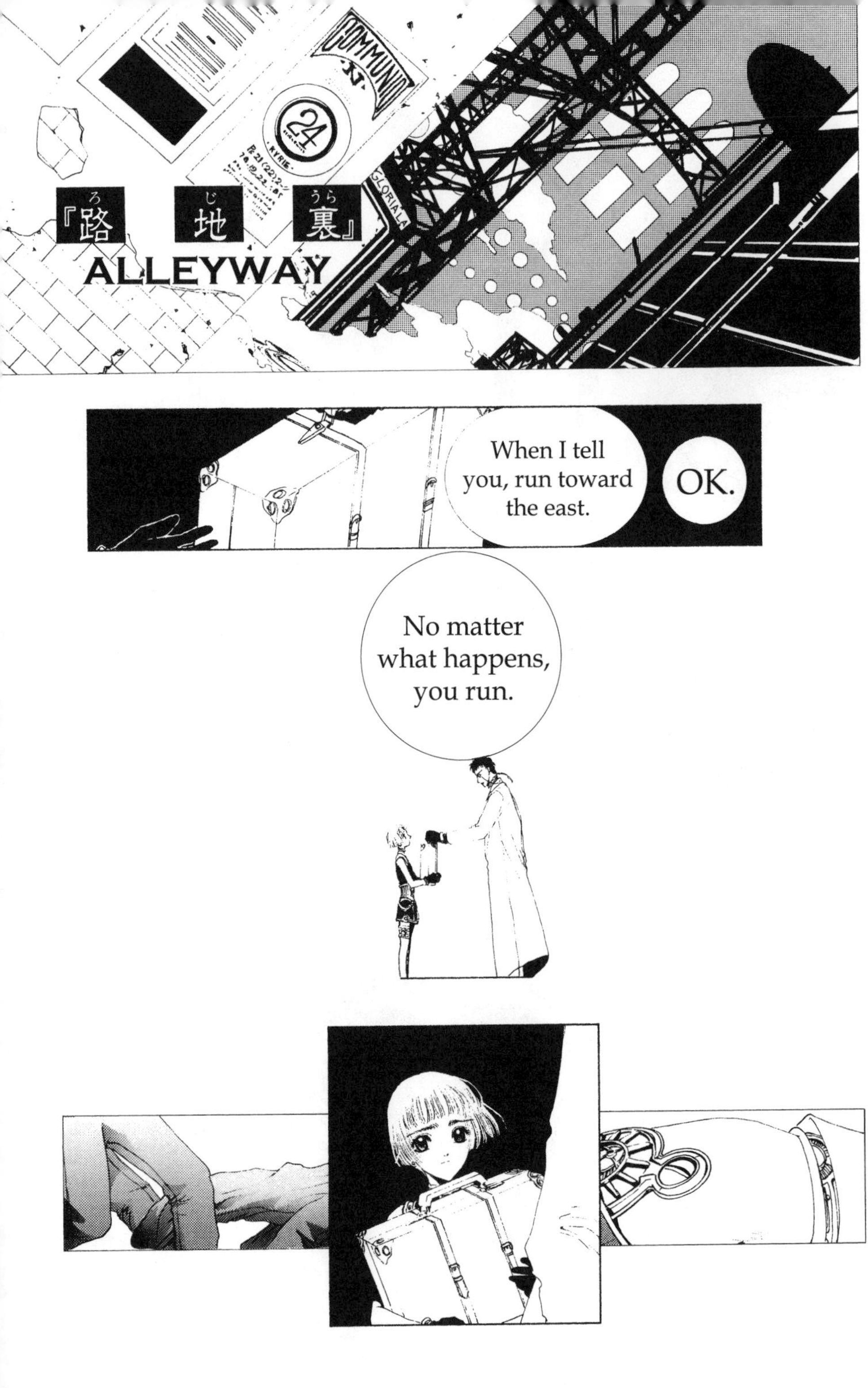
『路地裏』
ALLEYWAY
GLORIA LA
When I tell you, run toward the east.
OK.
No matter what happens, you run.

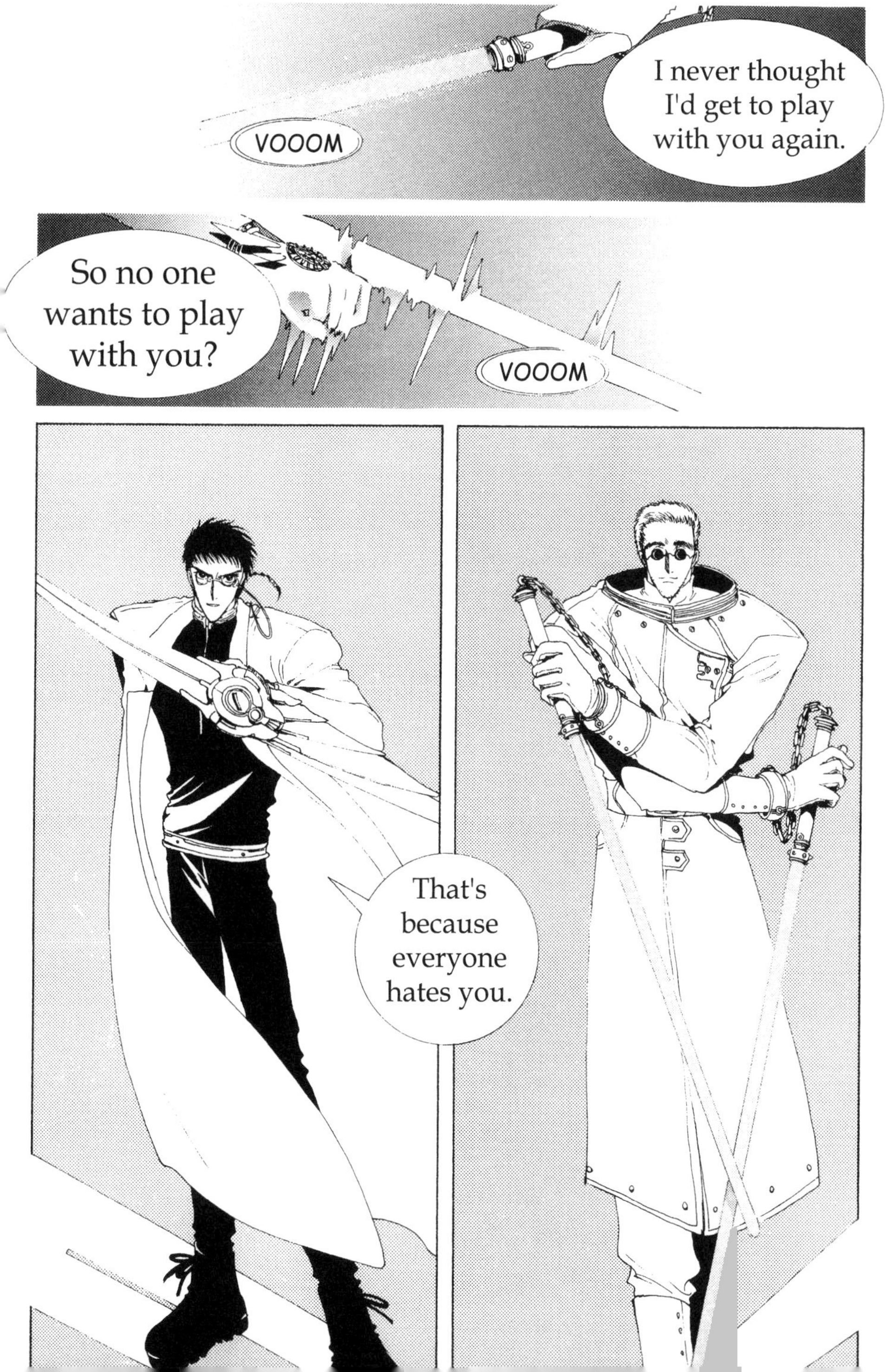
VOOOM
I never thought I'd get to play with you again.
So no one wants to play with you?
VOOOM
That's because everyone hates you.

That right hand of yours.

I've got it displayed in my bedroom.

I go to sleep with it every night.

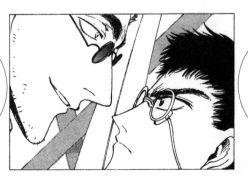

Doesn't that make you hard?

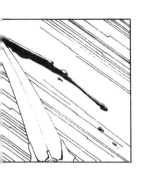

That's cute...

...my prince.

GGGGANK

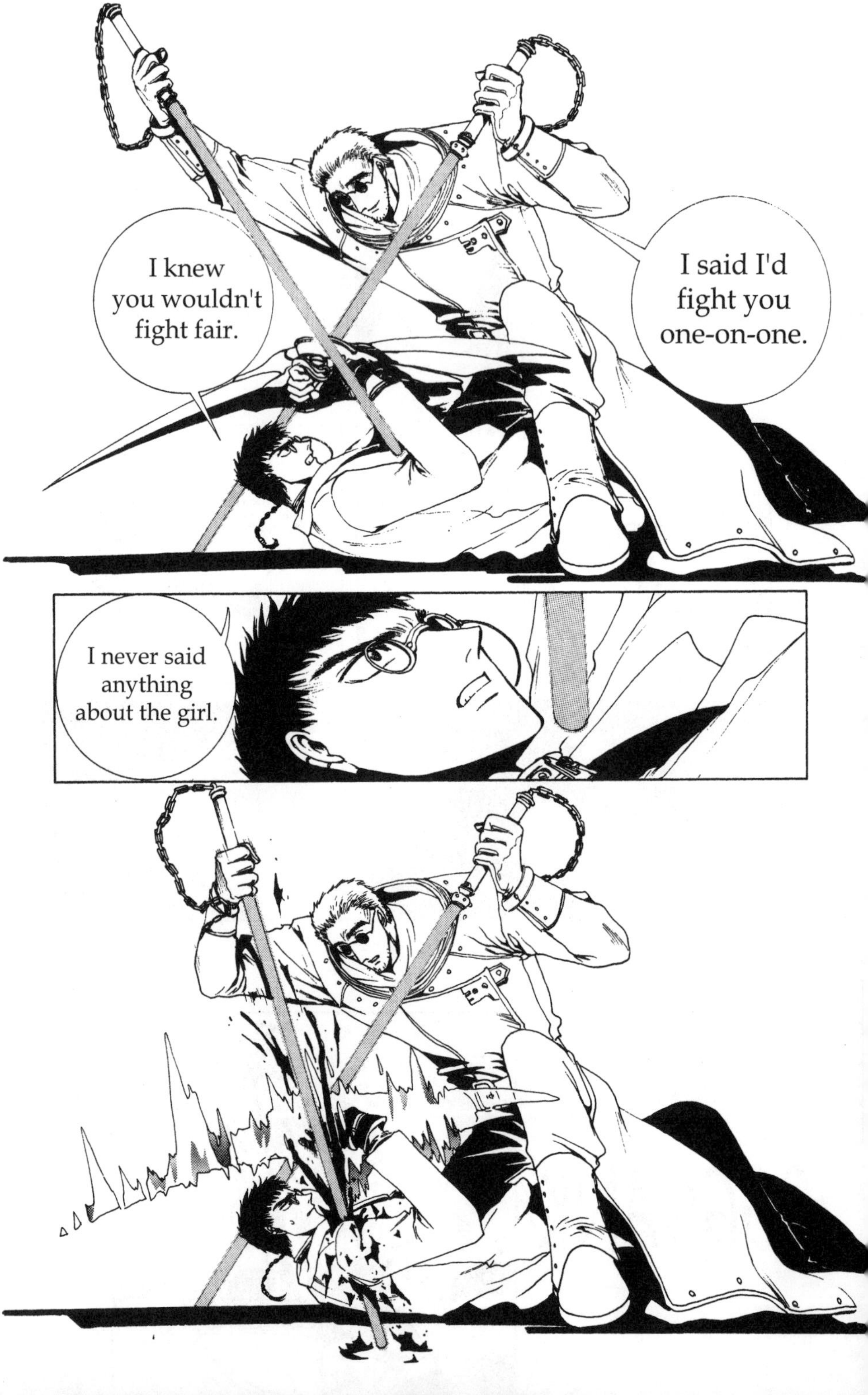
I knew you wouldn't fight fair.
I said I'd fight you one-on-one.
I never said anything about the girl.

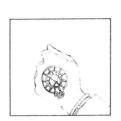

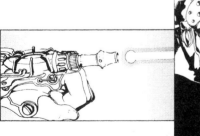

BEEEM

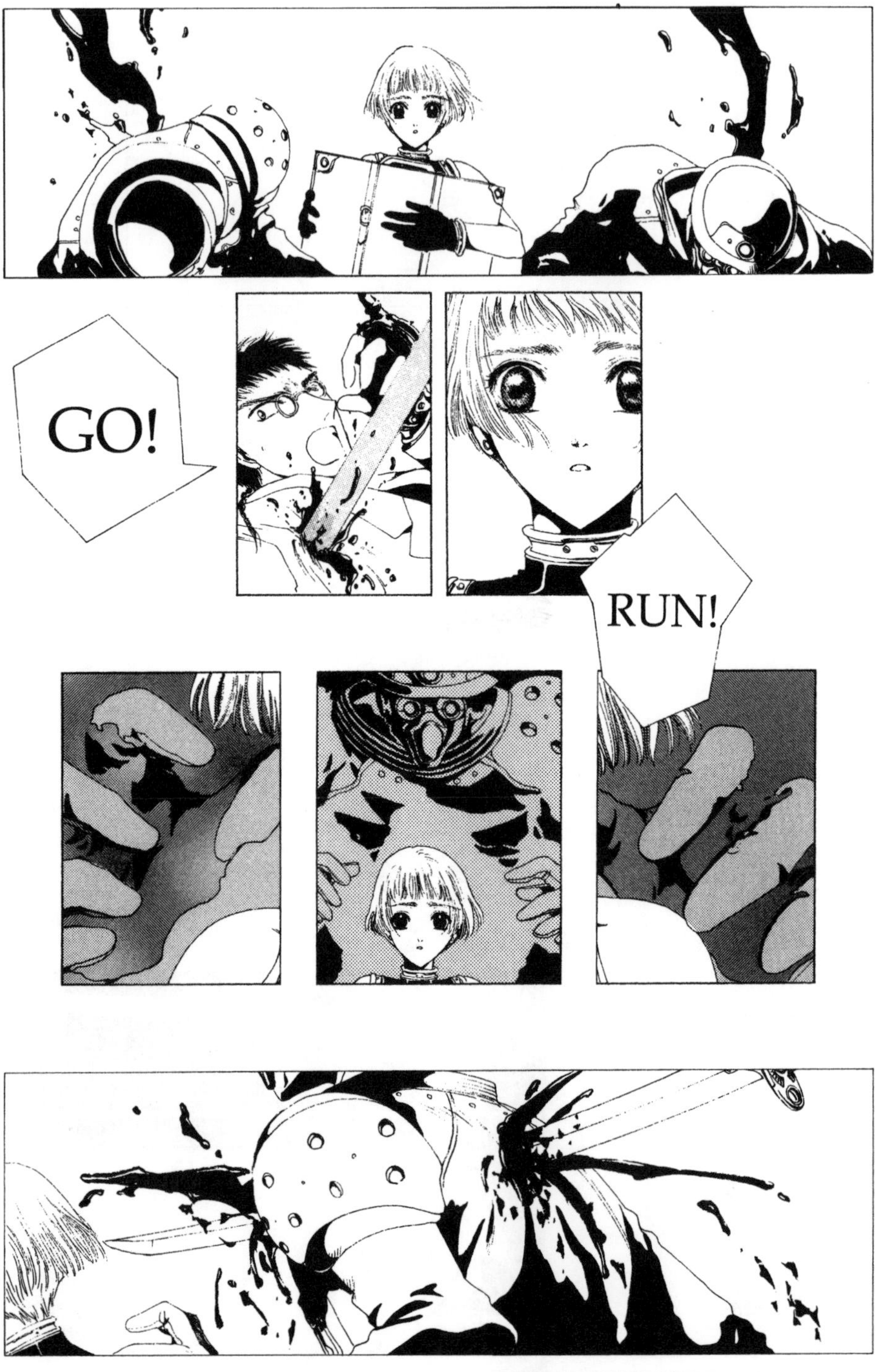
GO!
RUN!

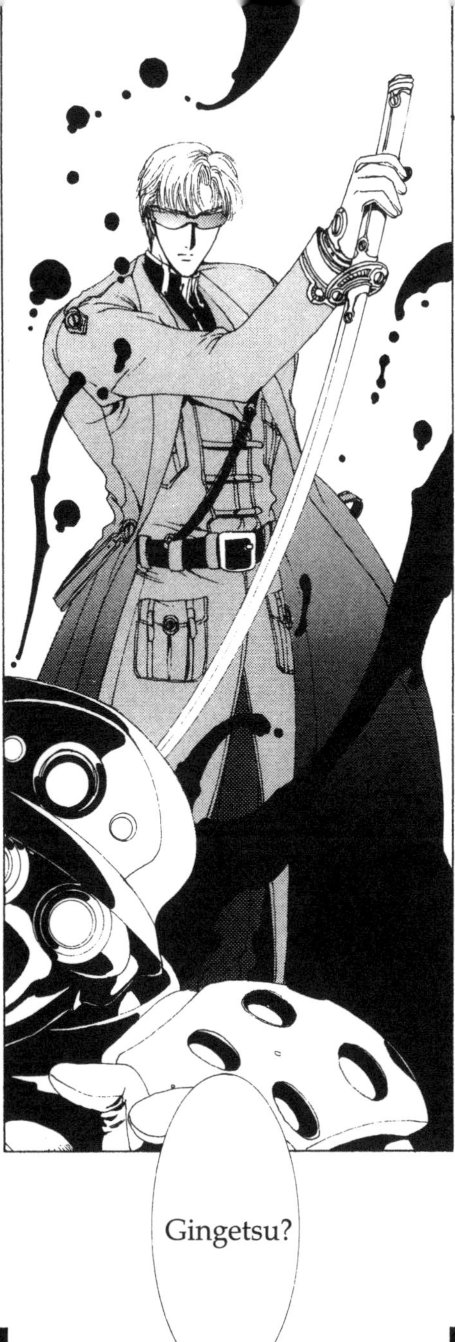
Gingetsu?

『傷痕』 THE SCAR

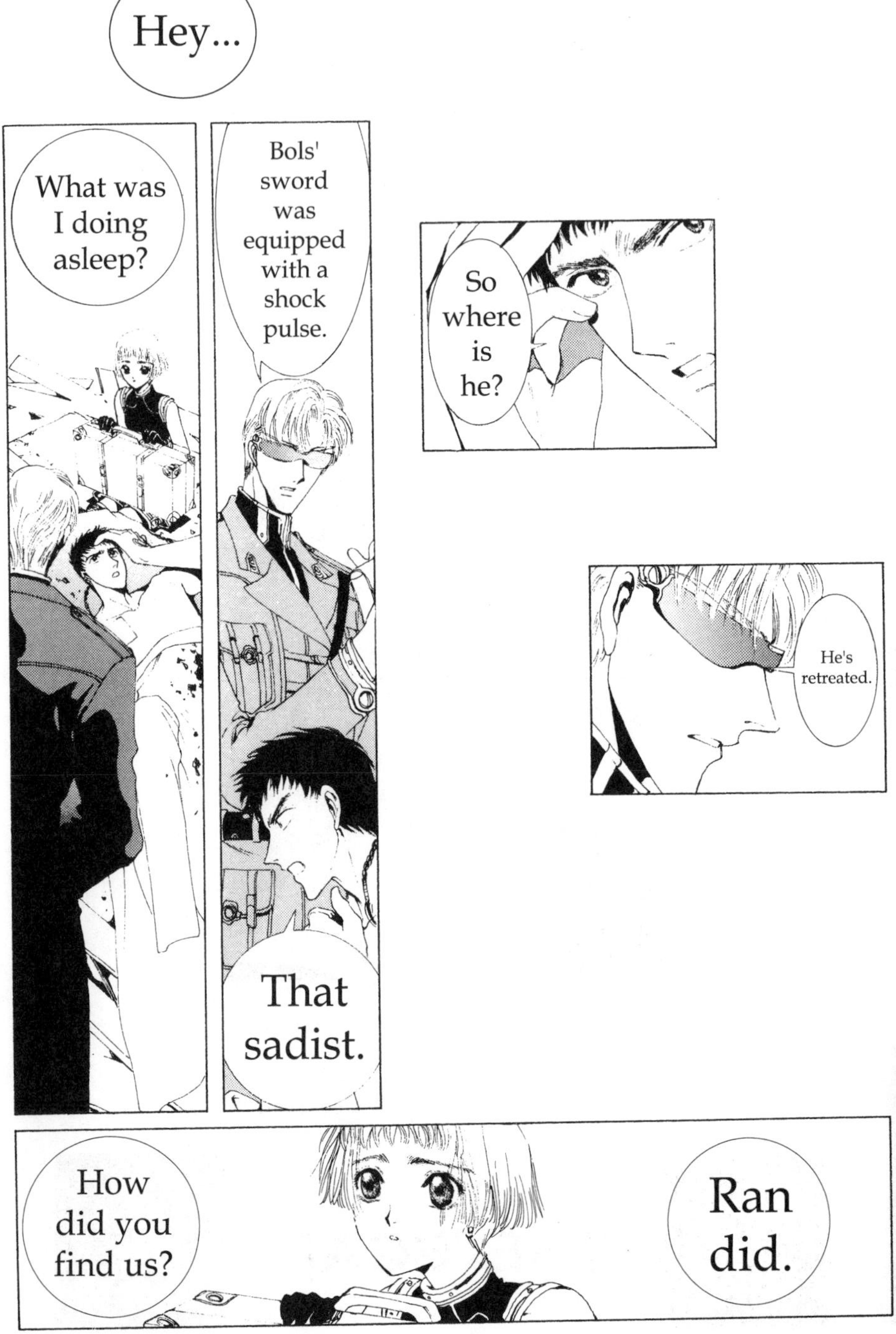
Hey...
What was I doing asleep?
Bols' sword was equipped with a shock pulse.
That sadist.
So where is he?
He's retreated.
How did you find us?
Ran did.

I hate the taste of these pain-killers.

Then don't take them.

Why didn't you run?

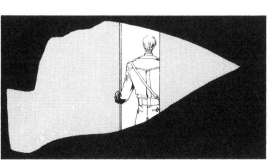

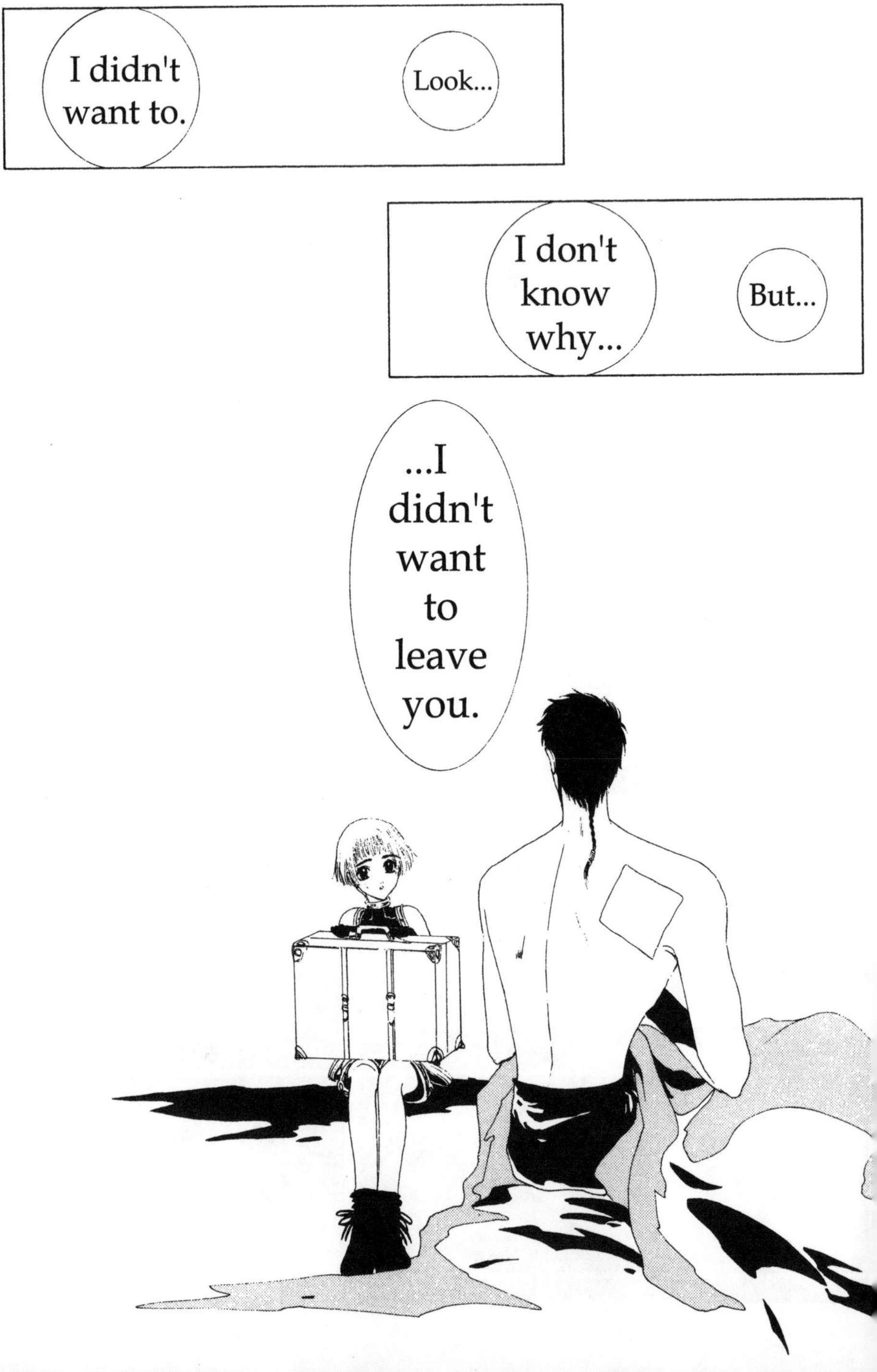
I didn't want to.
Look...
I don't know why...
But...
...I didn't want to leave you.

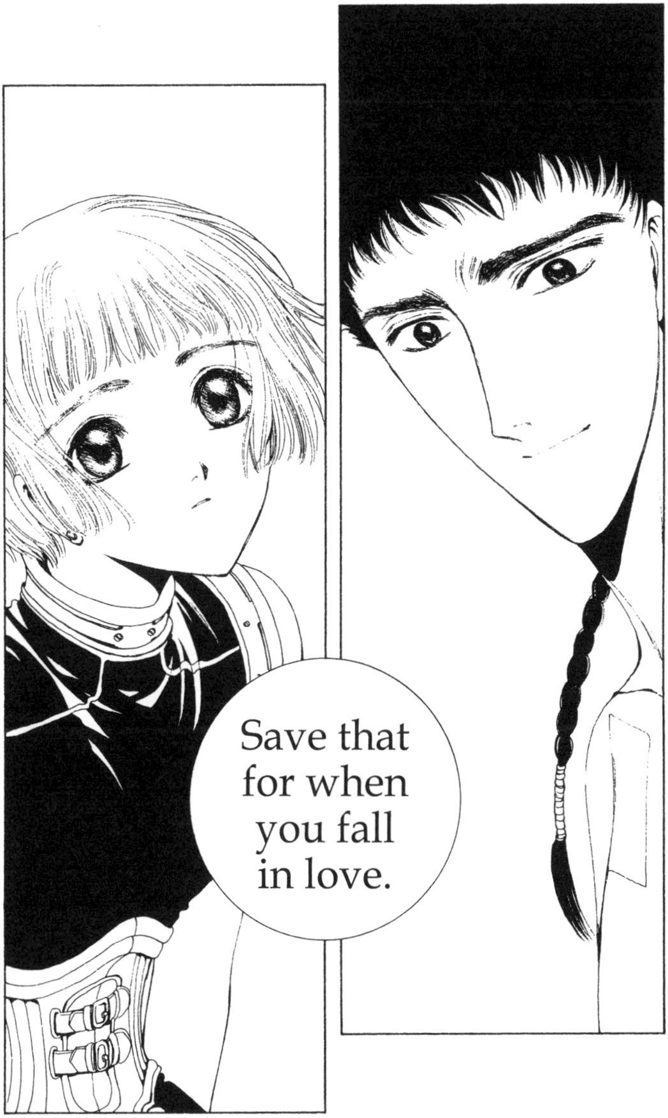
Save that for when you fall in love.

I
can't
say
that?

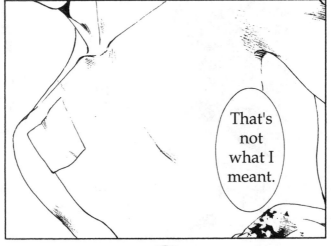

That's not what I meant.

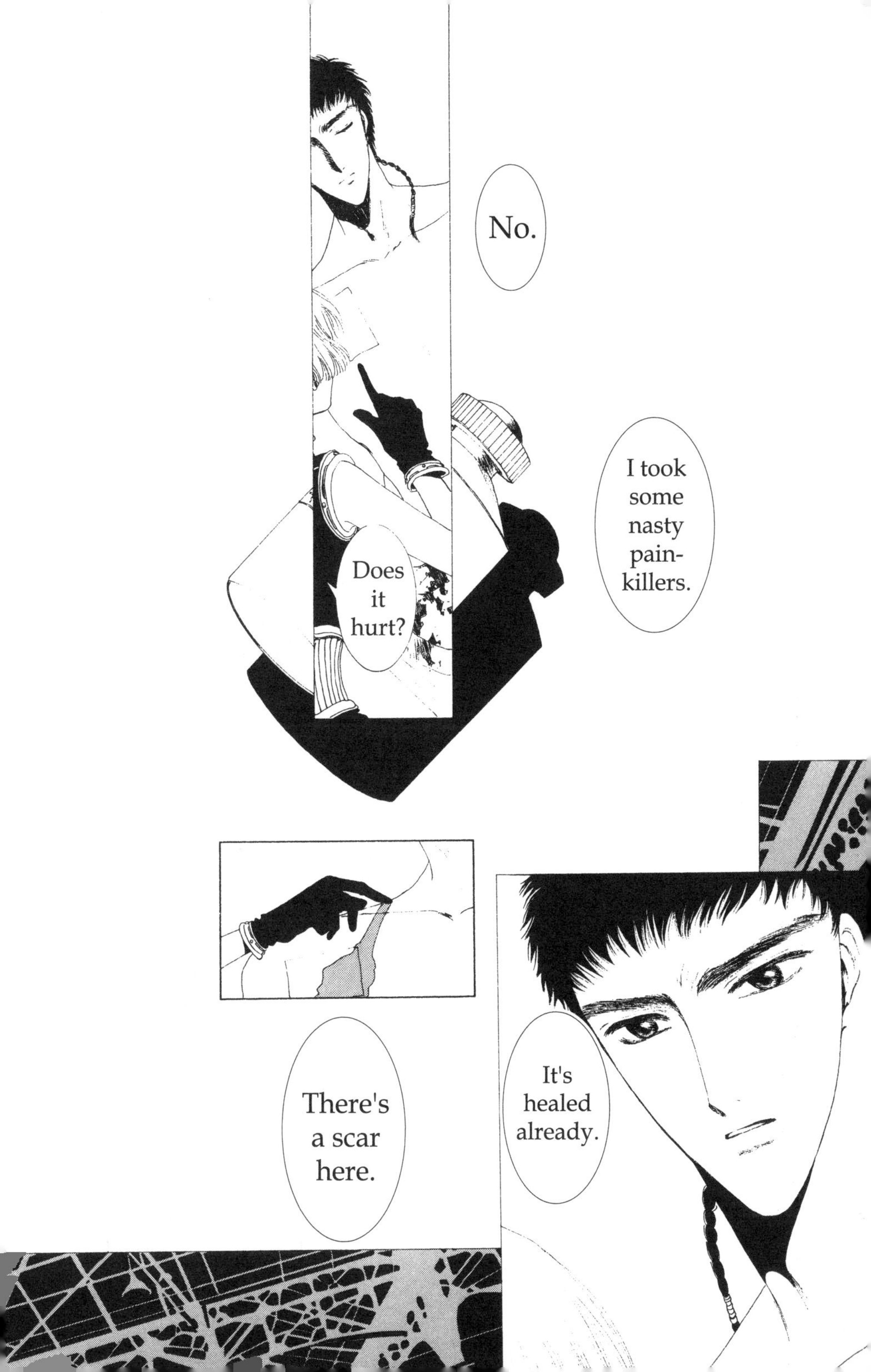
No.
Does it hurt?
I took some nasty pain-killers.
There's a scar here.
It's healed already.

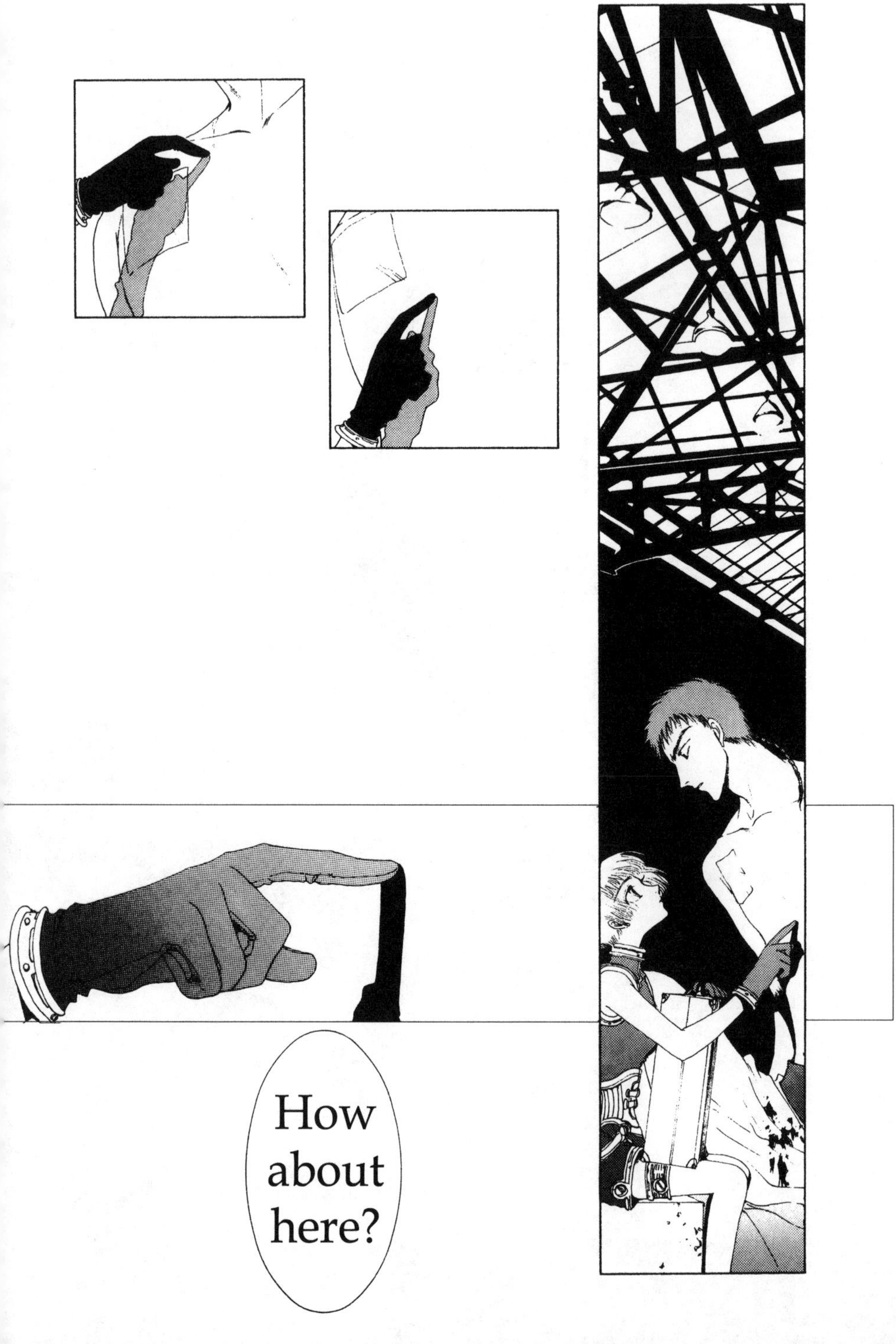
How about here?

Who
knows.

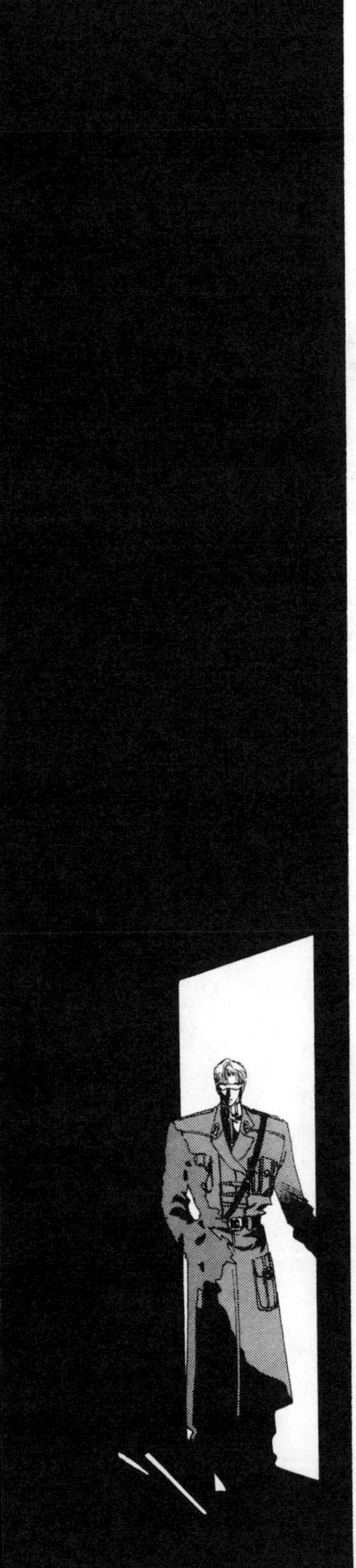

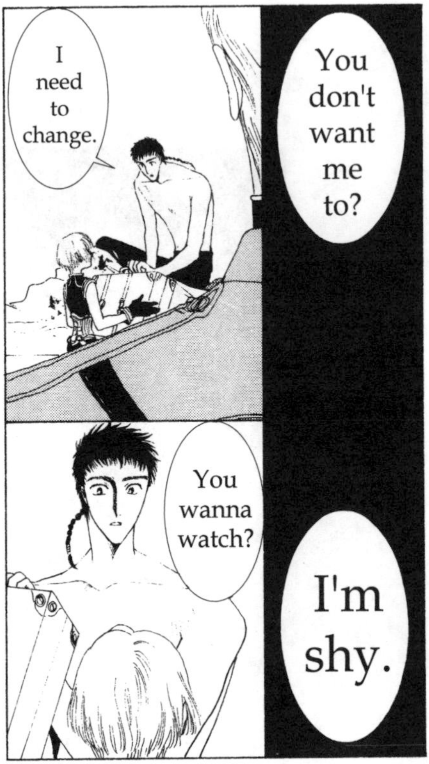
I need to change.
You wanna watch?
You don't want me to?
I'm shy.

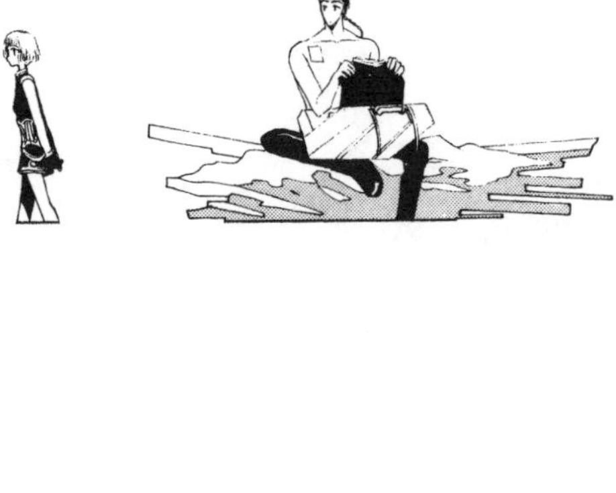

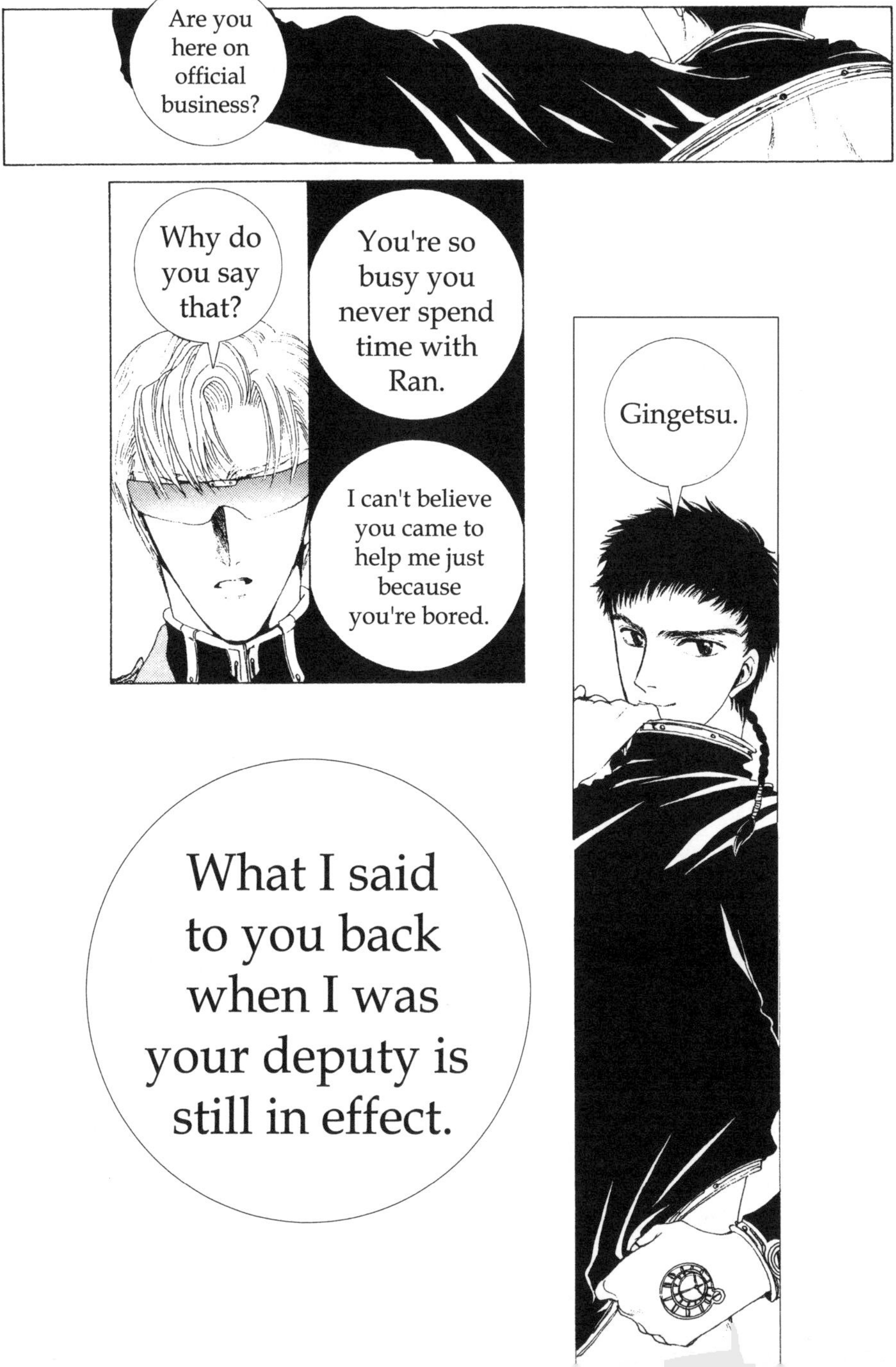
Are you here on official business?
Why do you say that?
You're so busy you never spend time with Ran.
I can't believe you came to help me just because you're bored.
What I said to you back when I was your deputy is still in effect.
Gingetsu.

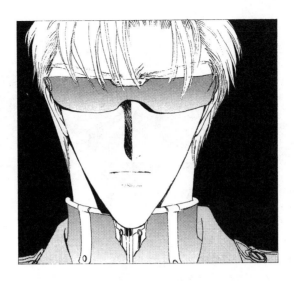

Bols is monitoring all public transport routes.

「歌」

A SONG

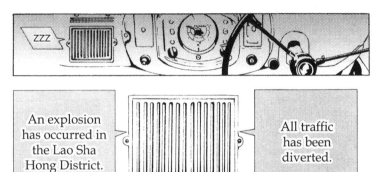

ZZZ

An explosion has occurred in the Lao Sha Hong District.

All traffic has been diverted.

Must be the Shiao Mao.

I wish for
happiness
I seek
happiness

So take me
Somewhere
far from here

I wish for
happiness
I seek
happiness

Take me
Somewhere
away from
here

Please
take me

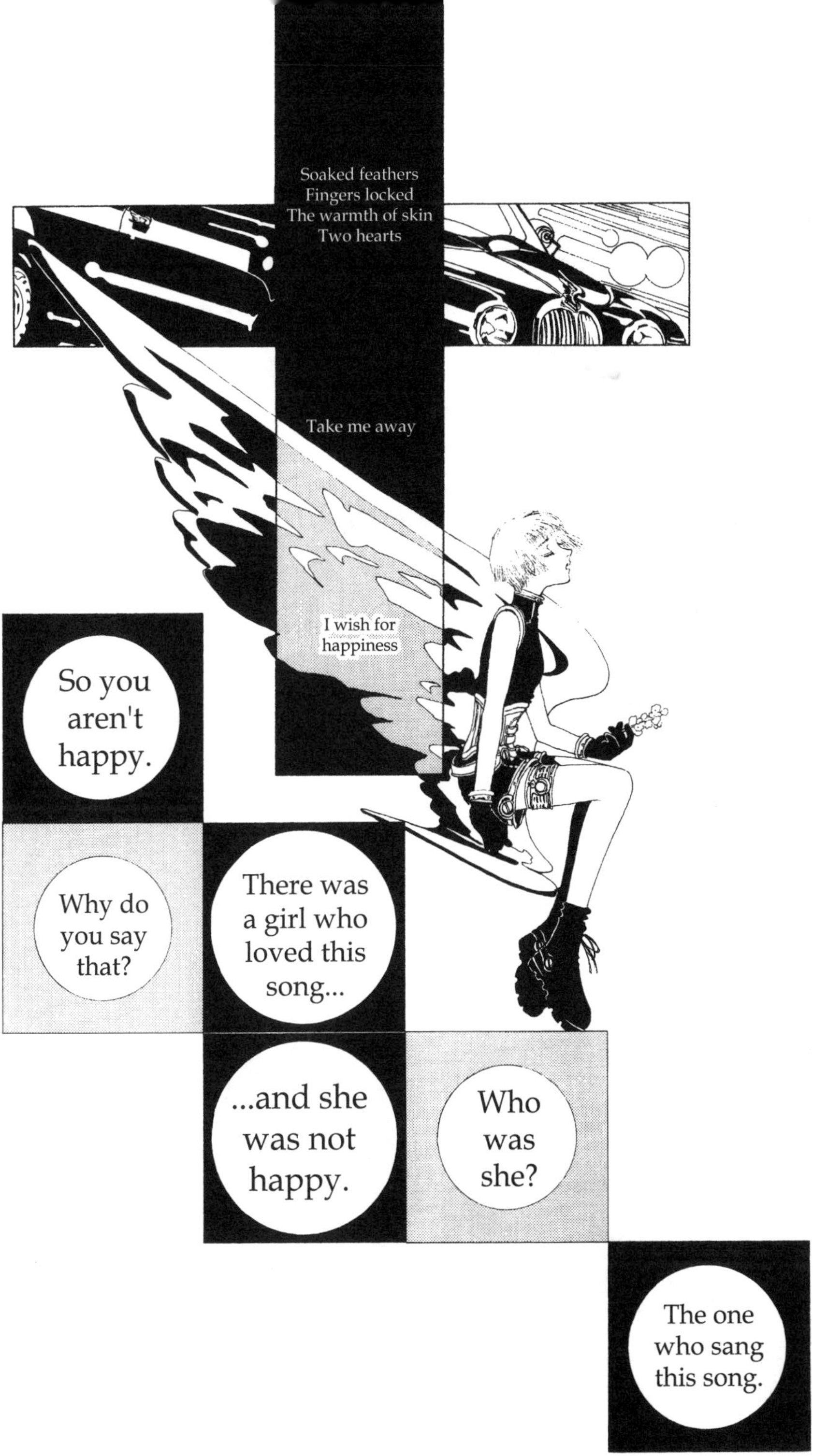
Soaked feathers
Fingers locked
The warmth of skin
Two hearts
Take me away
I wish for happiness
So you aren't happy.
Why do you say that?
There was a girl who loved this song...
...and she was not happy.
Who was she?
The one who sang this song.

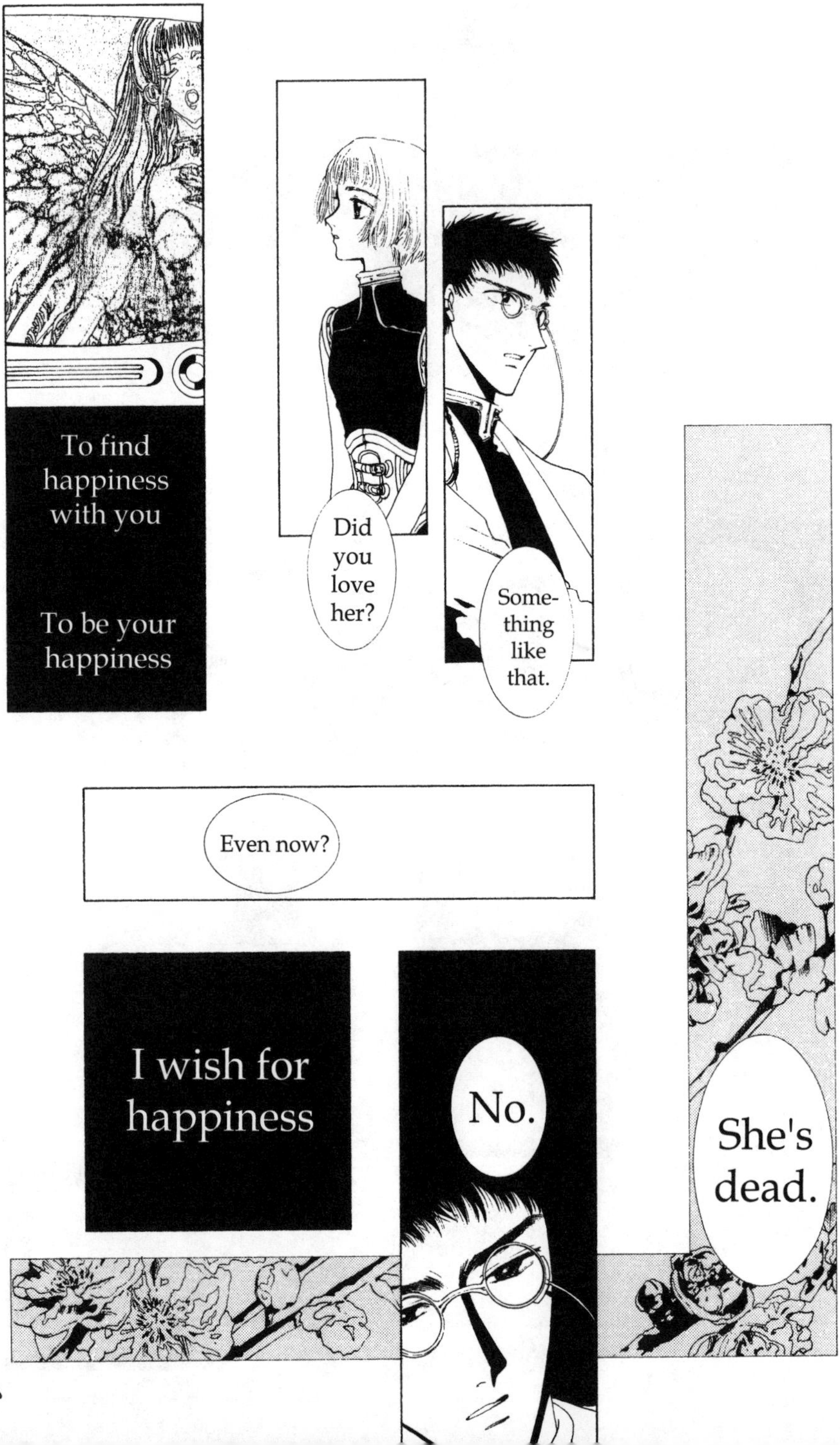
To find happiness with you
To be your happiness
Did you love her?
Something like that.
Even now?
I wish for happiness
No.
She's dead.

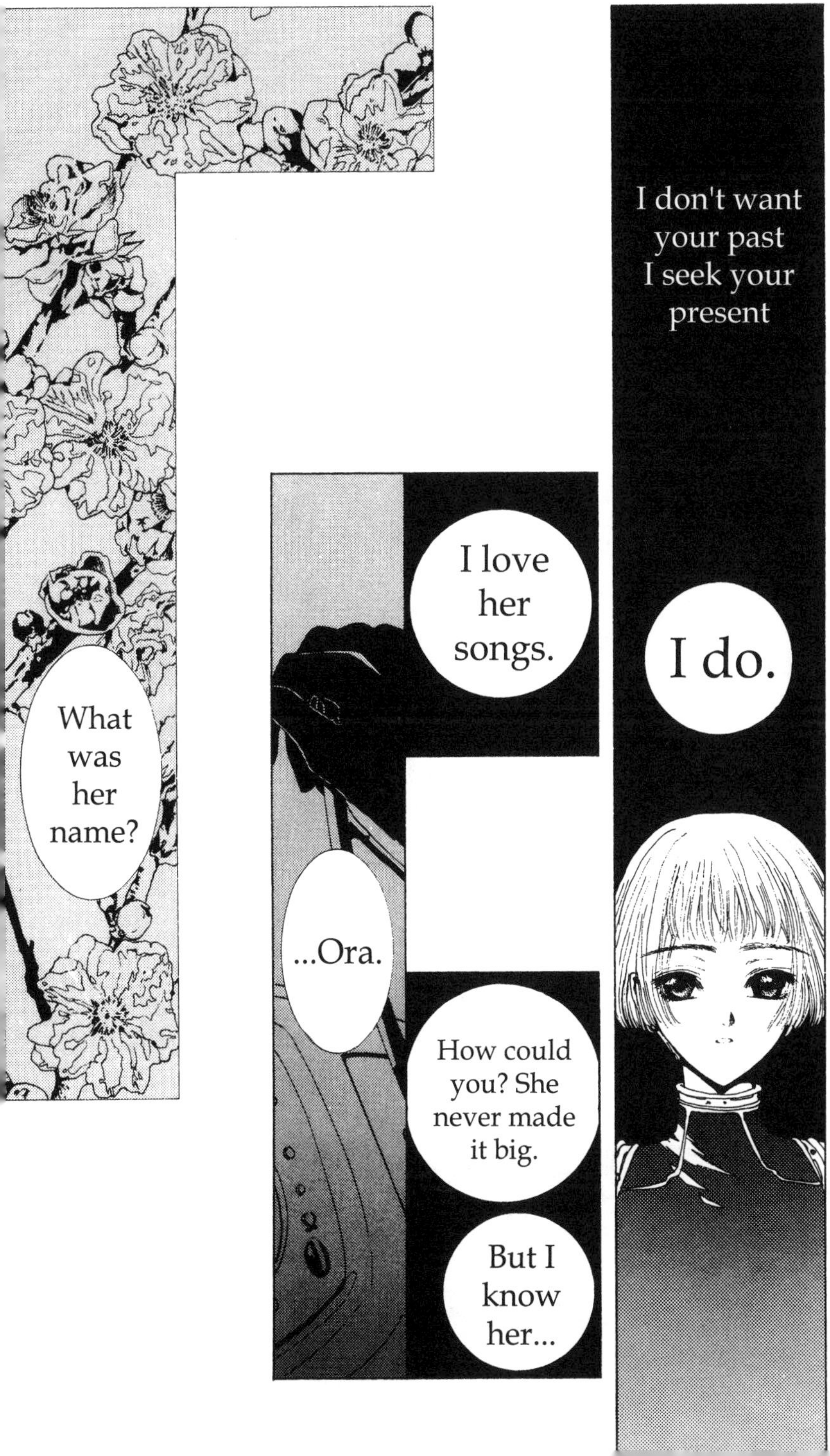
What was her name?
I love her songs.
...Ora.
How could you? She never made it big.
But I know her...
I don't want your past I seek your present
I do.

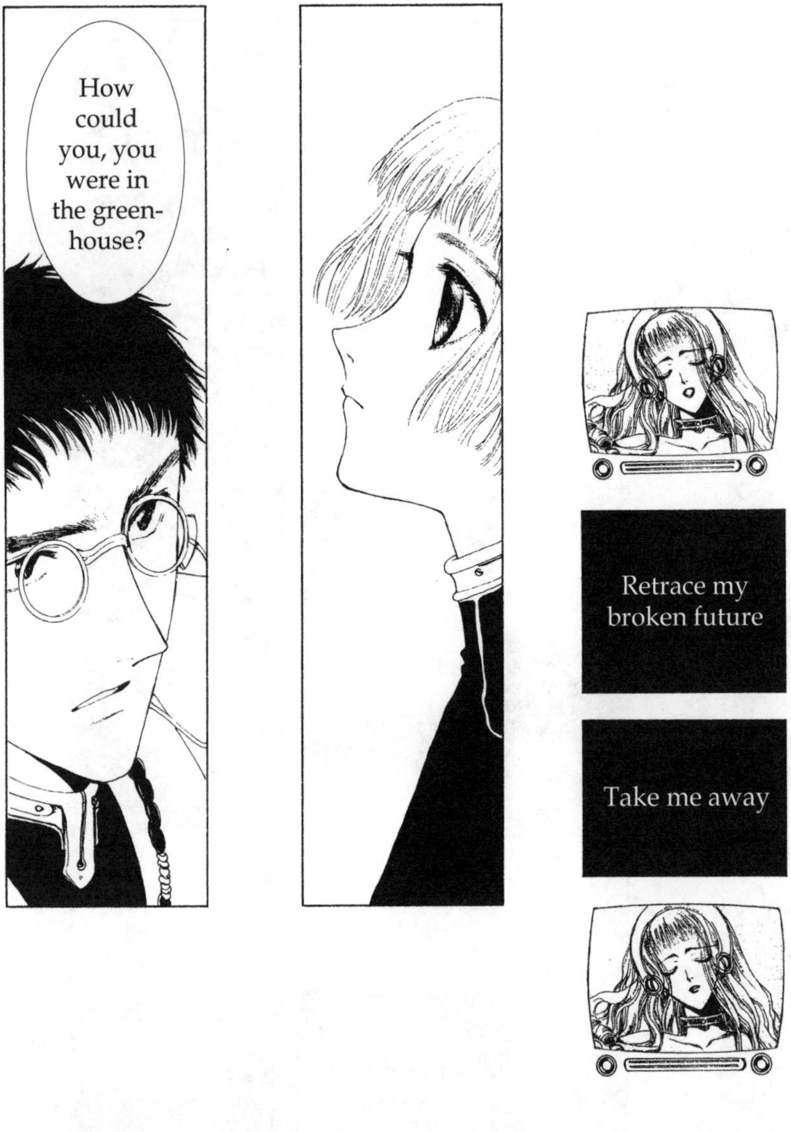
How could you, you were in the green-house?
Retrace my broken future
Take me away
I'm not happy now.
I haven't arrived at my destination yet.

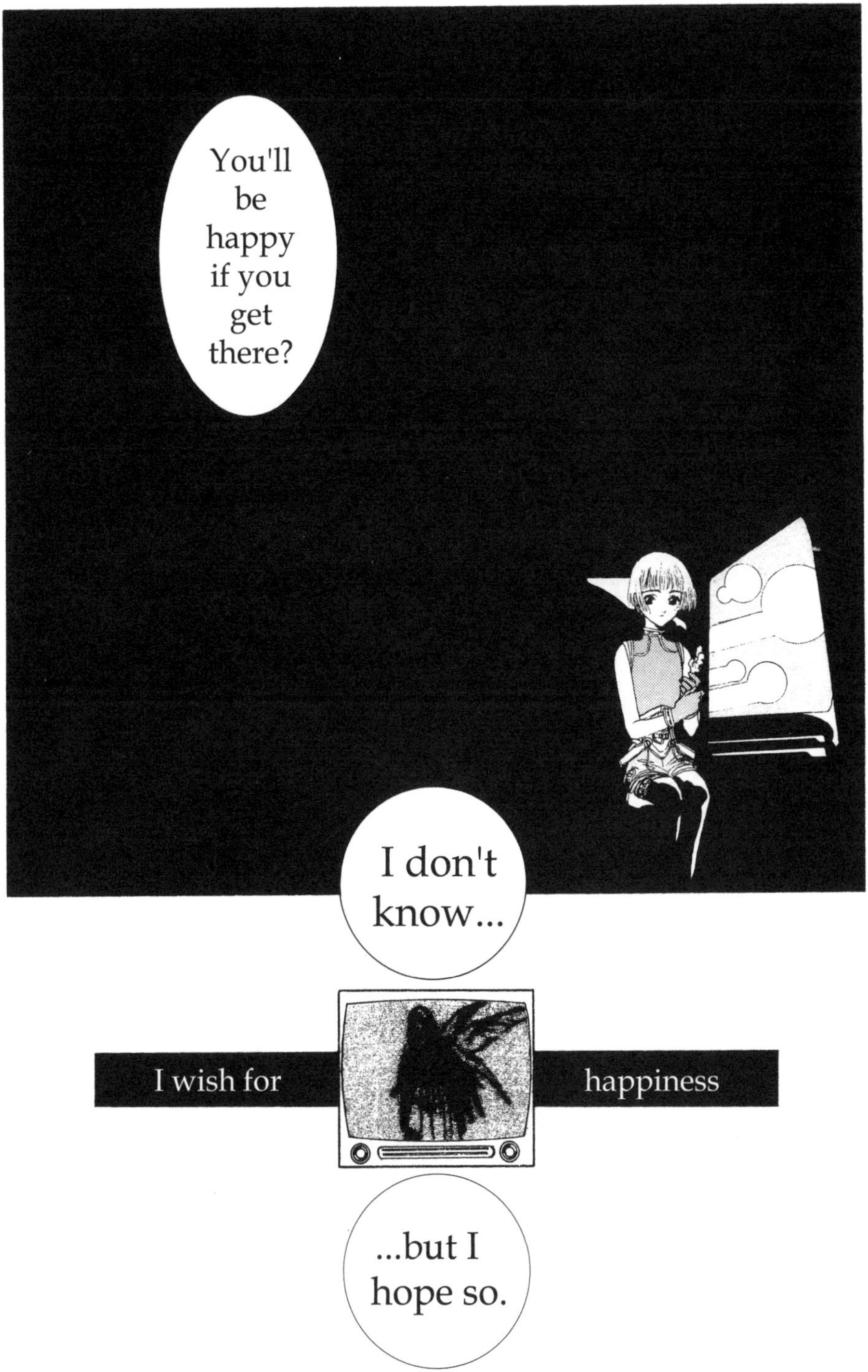
You'll be happy if you get there?
I don't know...
I wish for
happiness
...but I hope so.

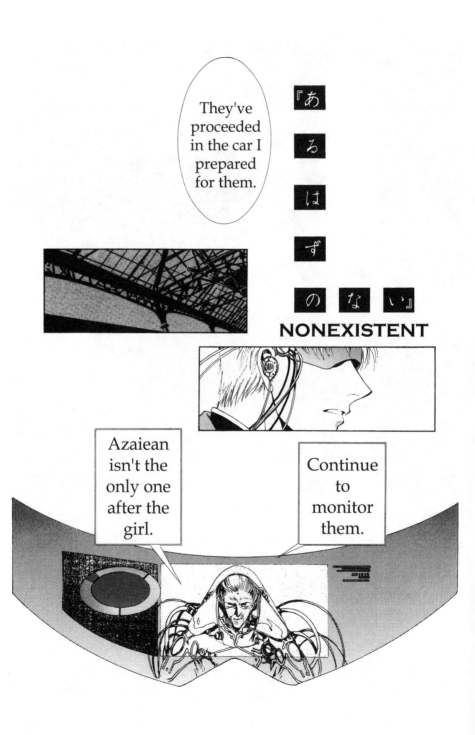

They've proceeded in the car I prepared for them.

『あるはずのない』

NONEXISTENT

Azaiean isn't the only one after the girl.

Continue to monitor them.

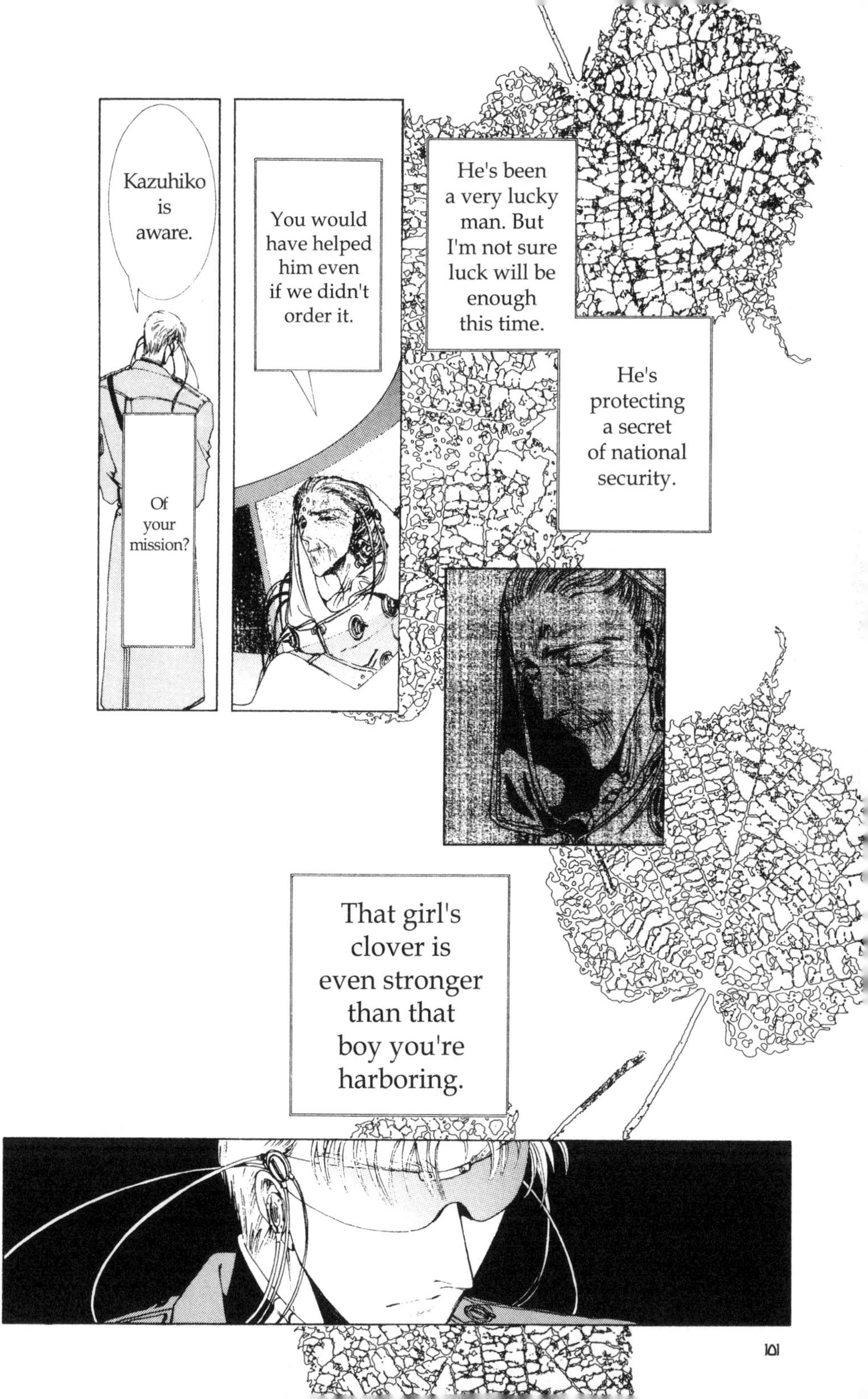

Kazuhiko is aware.
Of your mission?
You would have helped him even if we didn't order it.
He's been a very lucky man. But I'm not sure luck will be enough this time.
He's protecting a secret of national security.
That girl's clover is even stronger than that boy you're harboring.

I never
knew it
existed
until now.
A four-
leaf
clover.

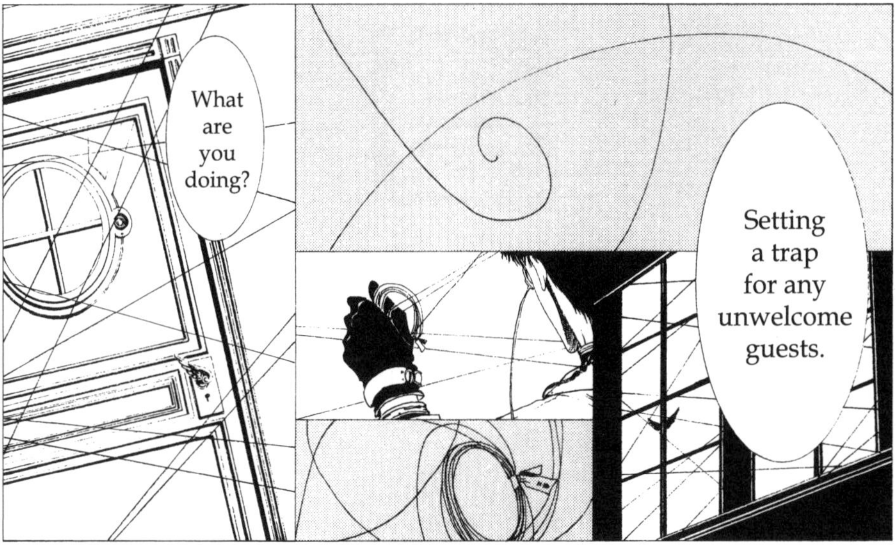
What are you doing?
Setting a trap for any unwelcome guests.

GOODNIGHT

『おやすみ』

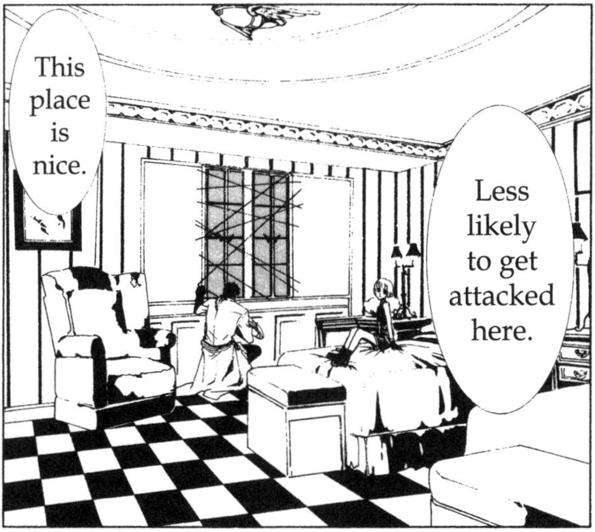
This place is nice.
Less likely to get attacked here.

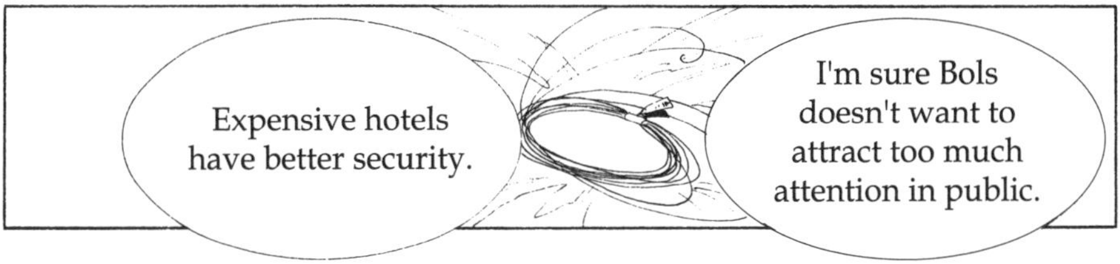
Expensive hotels have better security.
I'm sure Bols doesn't want to attract too much attention in public.

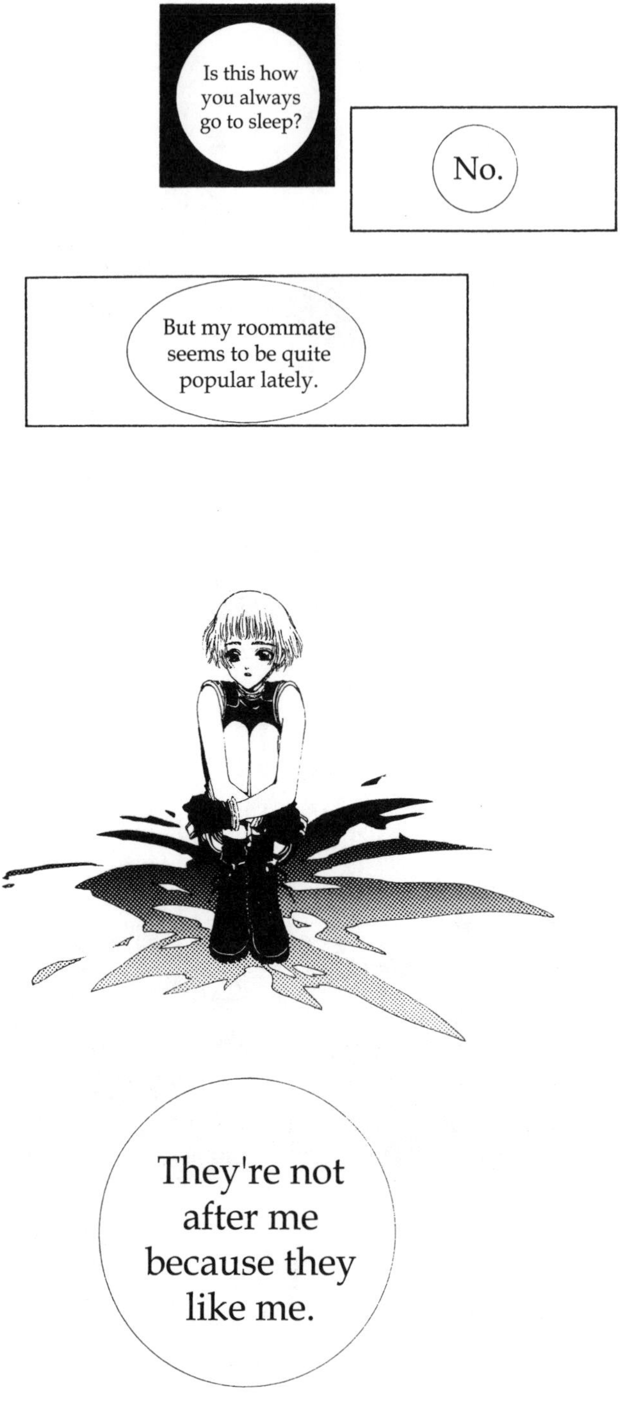
Is this how you always go to sleep?
No.
But my roommate seems to be quite popular lately.
They're not after me because they like me.

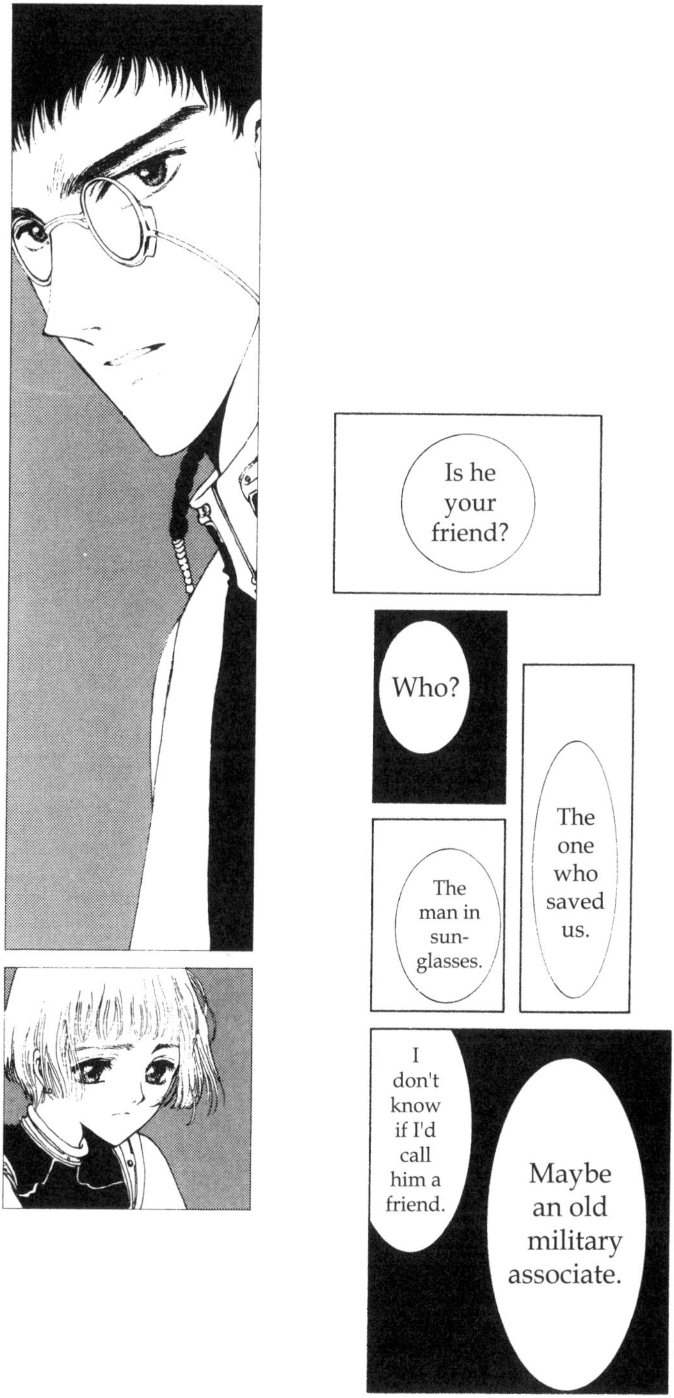
Is he your friend?
Who?
The man in sun-glasses.
The one who saved us.
I don't know if I'd call him a friend.
Maybe an old military associate.

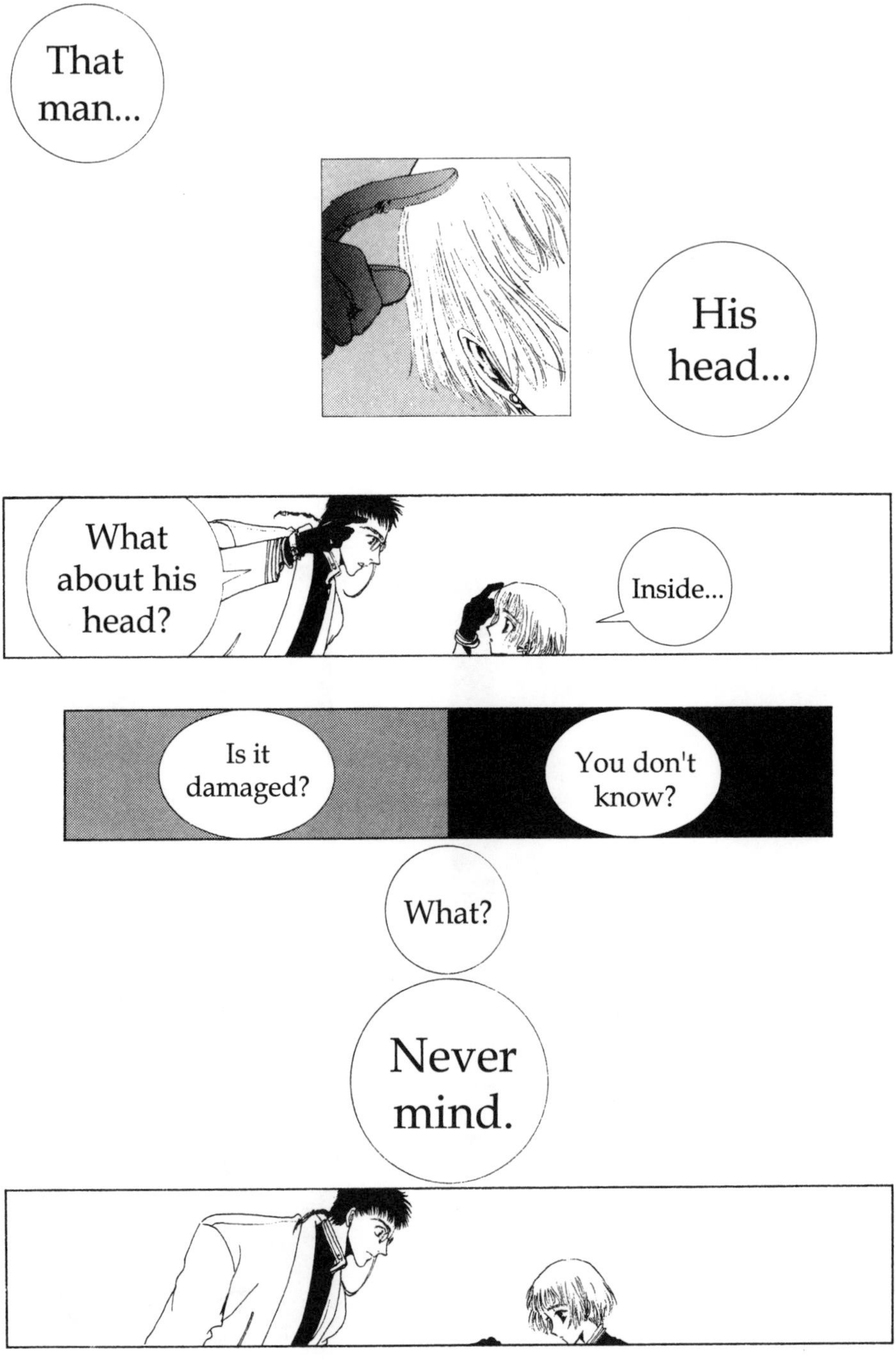
That man...
His head...
What about his head?
Inside...
Is it damaged?
You don't know?
What?
Never mind.

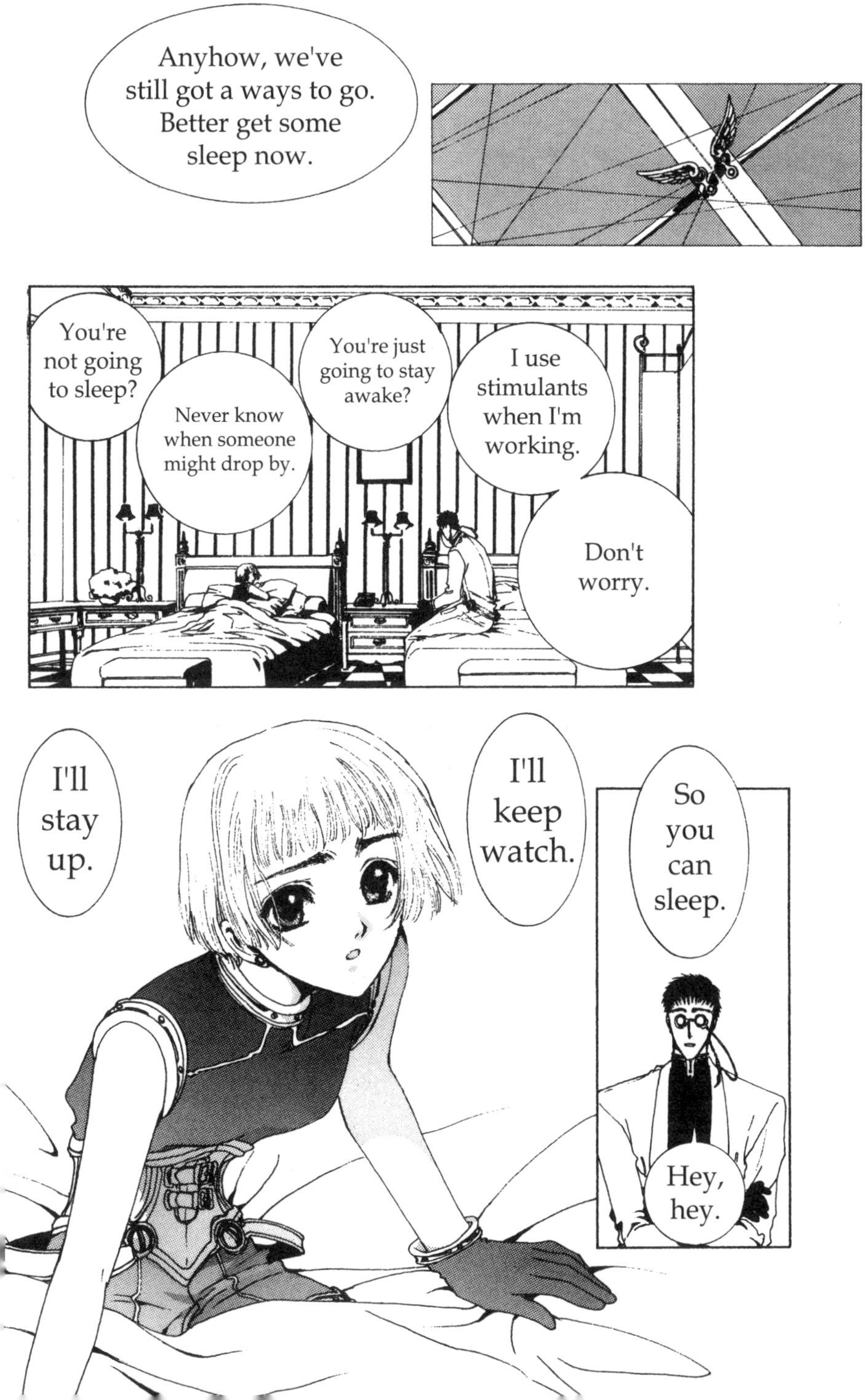
Anyhow, we've still got a ways to go. Better get some sleep now.
You're not going to sleep?
Never know when someone might drop by.
You're just going to stay awake?
I use stimulants when I'm working.
Don't worry.
I'll stay up.
I'll keep watch.
So you can sleep.
Hey, hey.

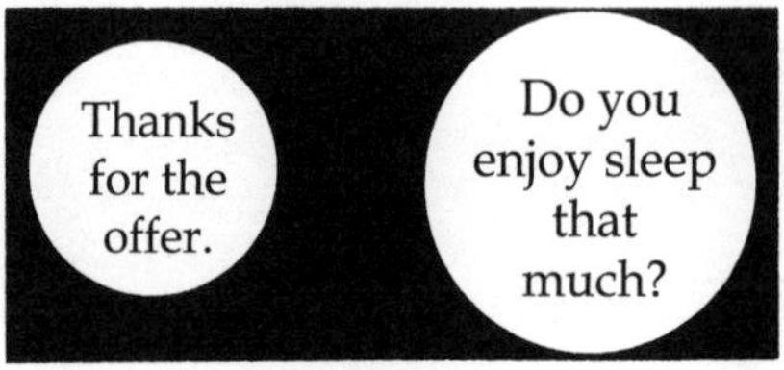
Thanks for the offer.
Do you enjoy sleep that much?

I can forget when I'm asleep...

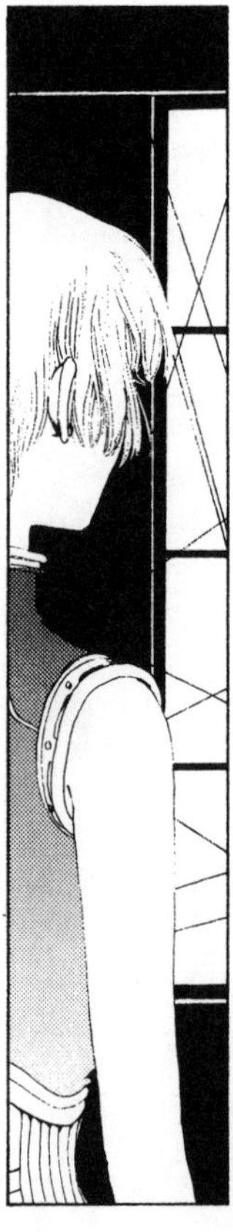

Forget
I'm
alone.

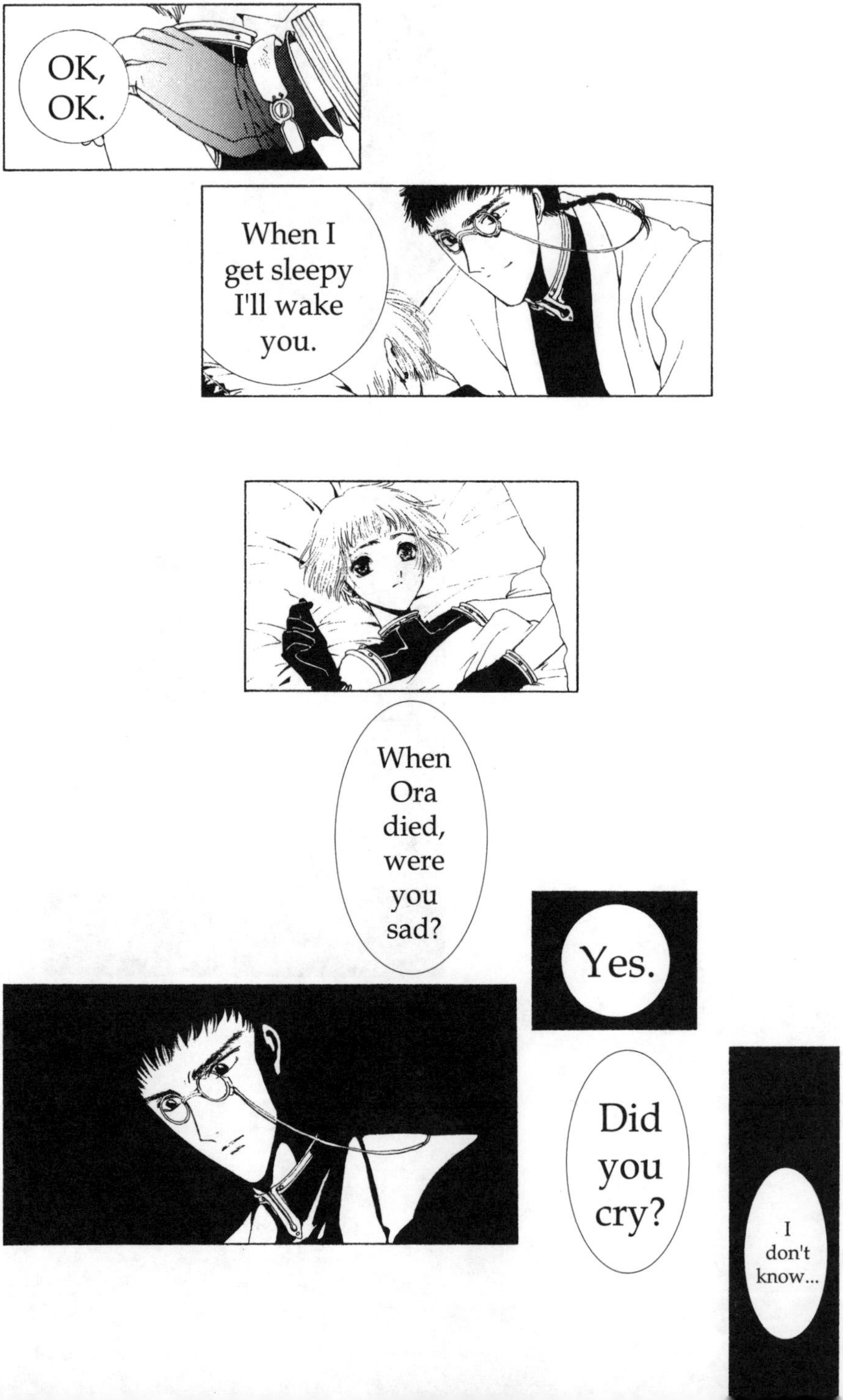
OK, OK.
When I get sleepy I'll wake you.
When Ora died, were you sad?
Yes.
Did you cry?
I don't know...

When I die, nobody will cry for me.

Why?

Because I'm alone.

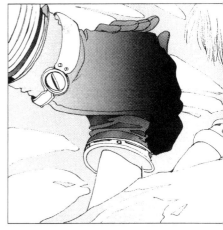

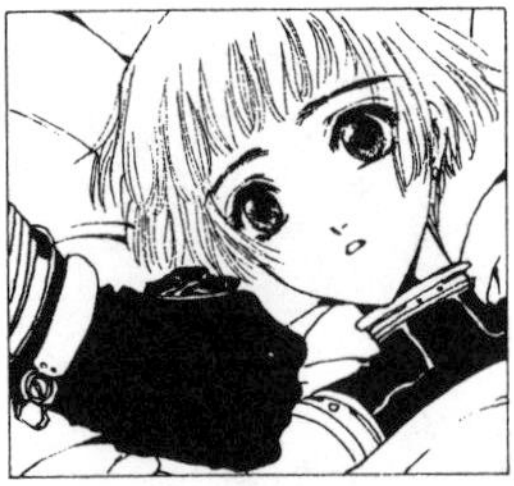

She had a very gentle voice.

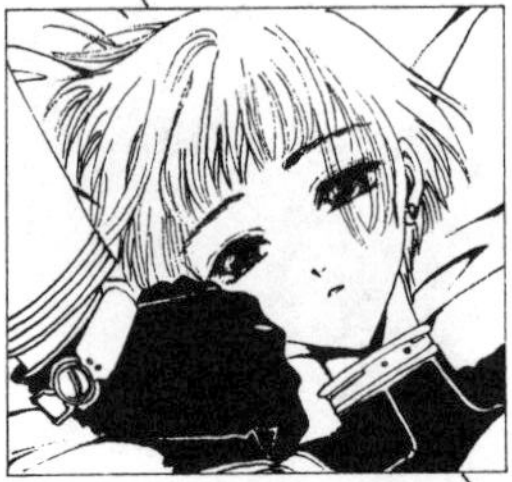

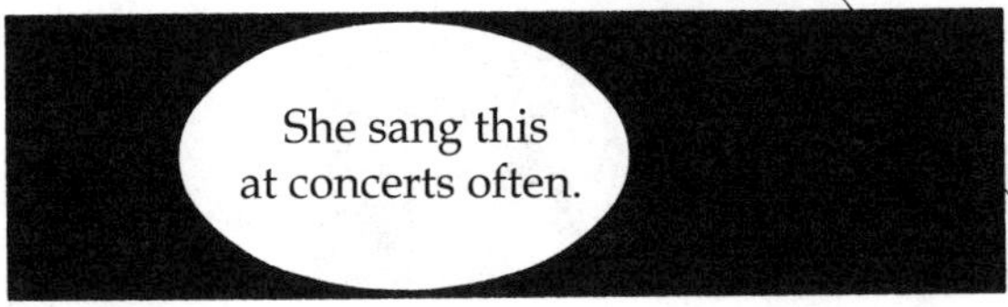
She sang this at concerts often.

Soaked feathers
Fingers locked
The warmth of skin
Two hearts

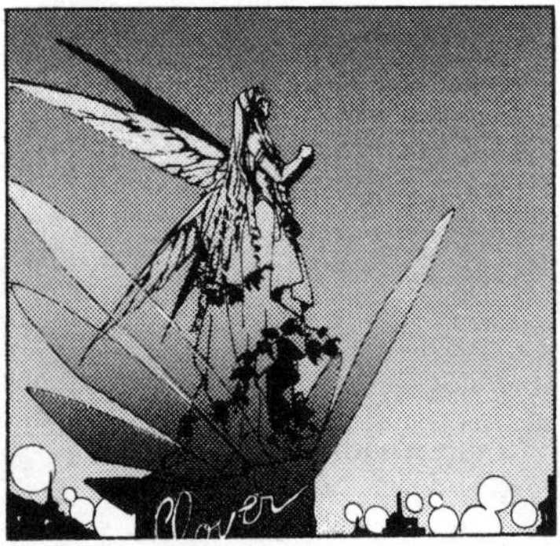
Clover

Take me away
I wish for
happiness

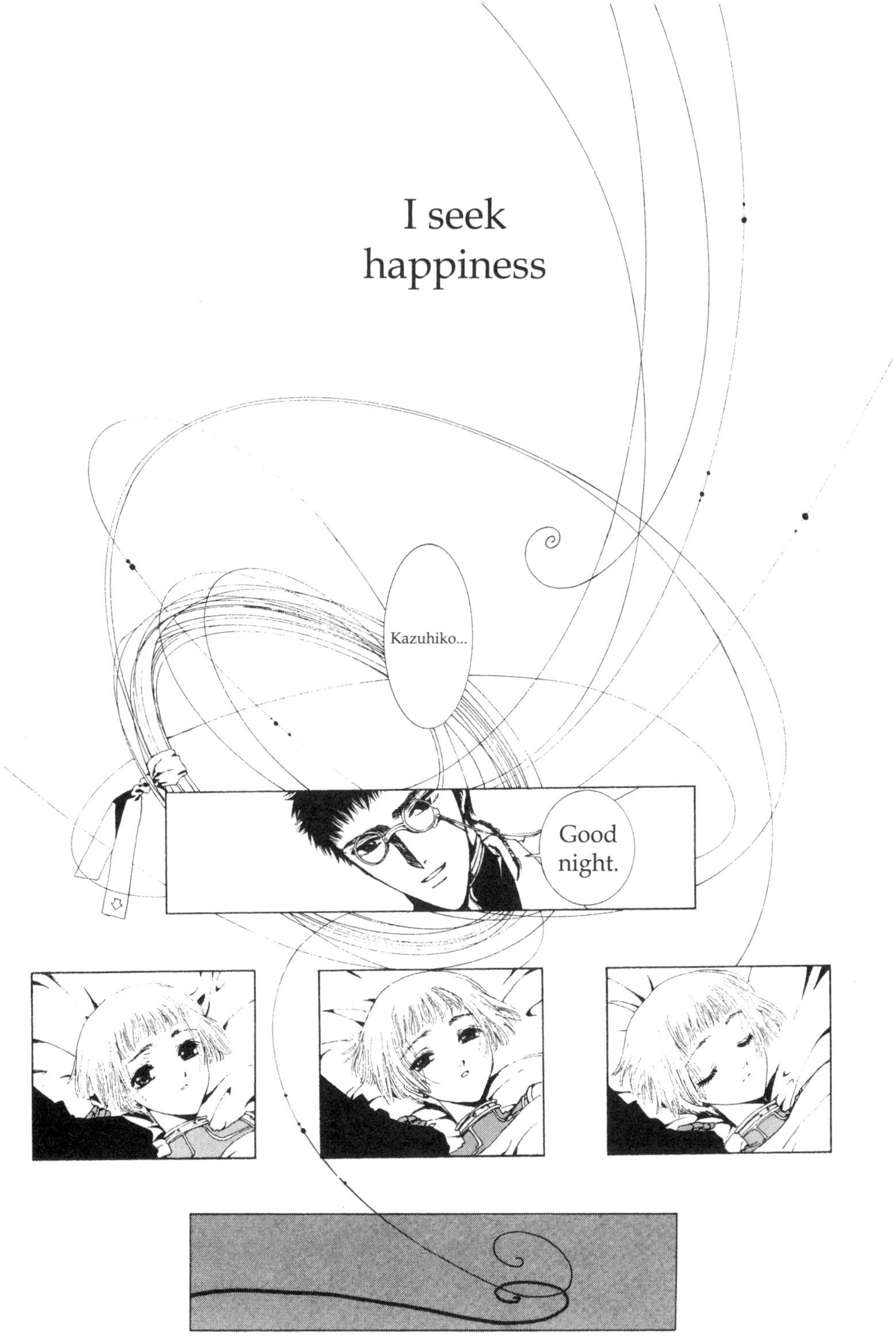
I seek happiness
Kazuhiko...
Good night.

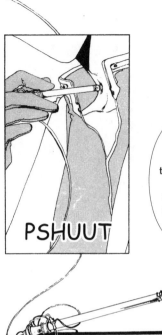

PSHUUT

We need
to get there
before I
run out of
stimulant.

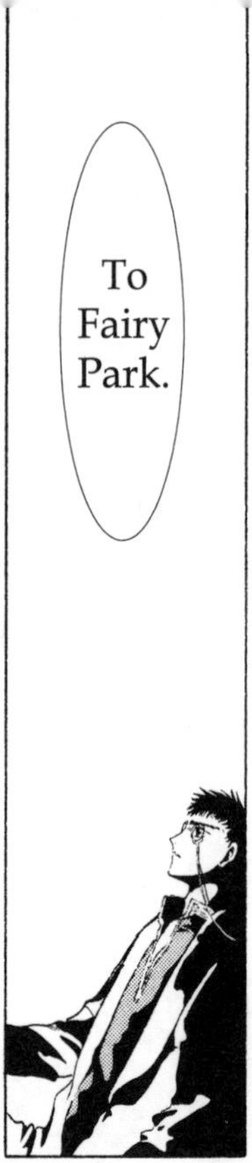

To
Fairy
Park.

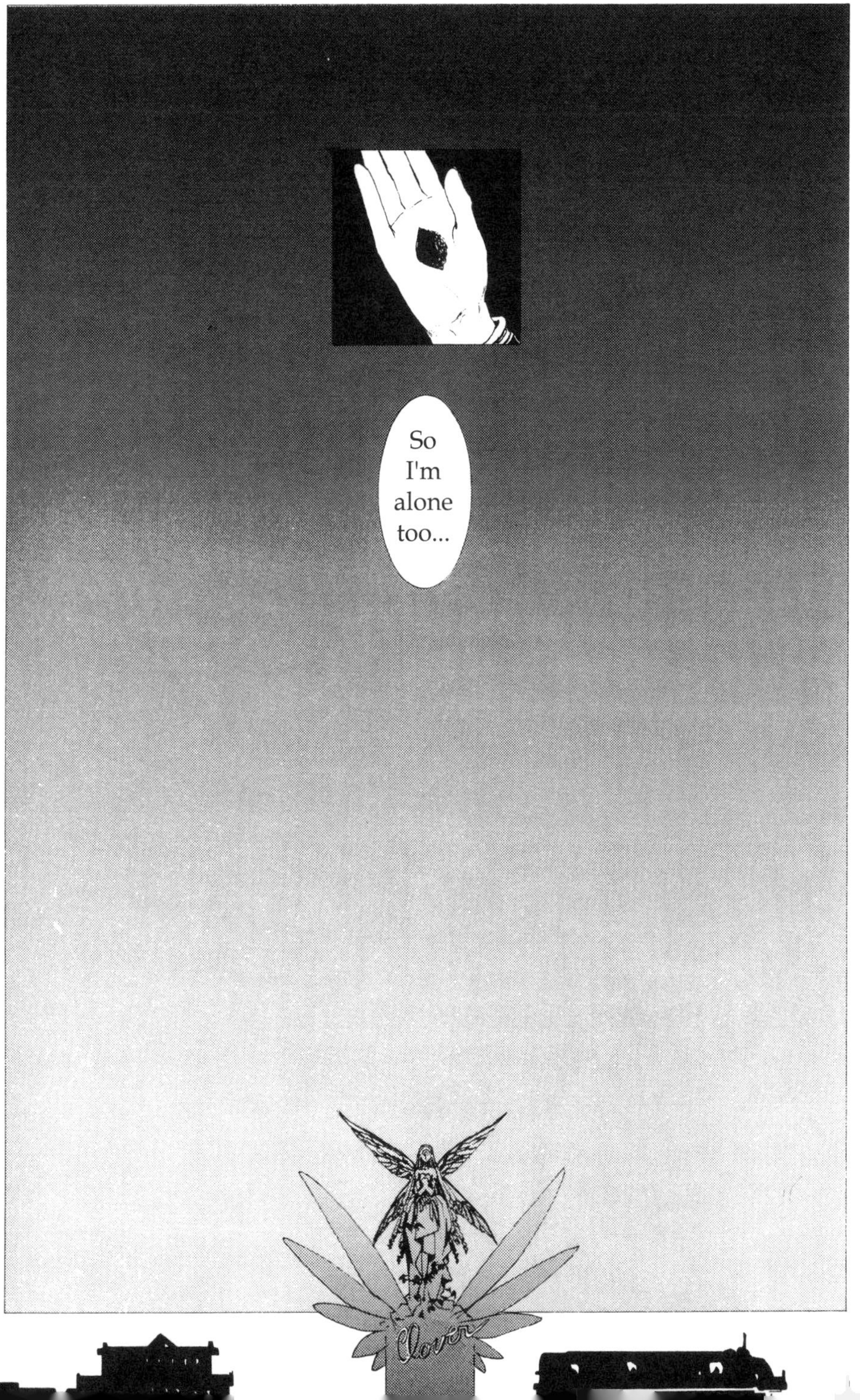

So I'm alone too...
Clover

PURSUIT

Here comes Gingetsu.

I was thinking that Kazuhiko might be a decoy.

But if Commander Gingetsu of Secret Operations is here...

...then it must be the real thing.

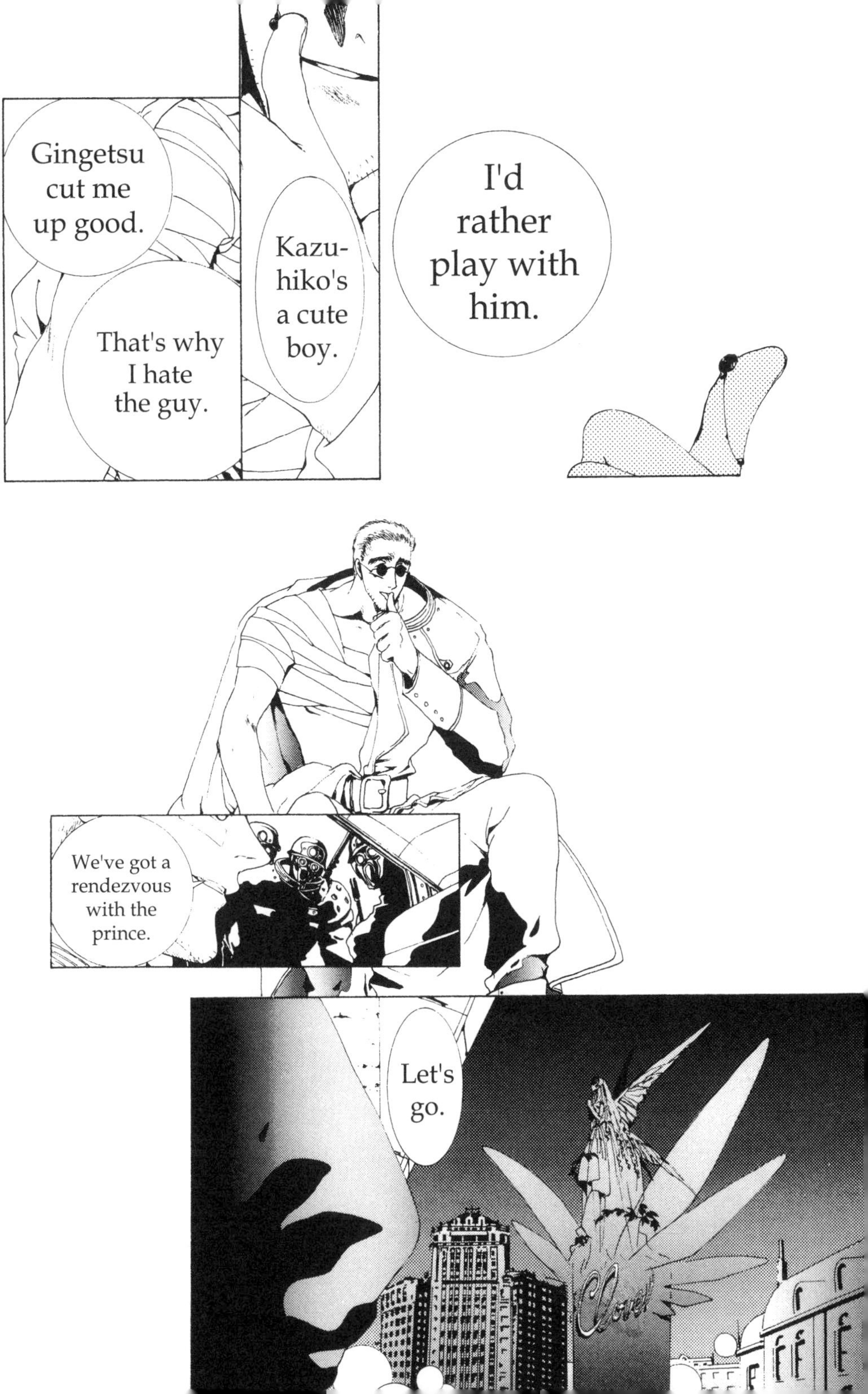
Gingetsu cut me up good.
That's why I hate the guy.
Kazuhiko's a cute boy.
I'd rather play with him.
We've got a rendezvous with the prince.
Let's go.
Clover

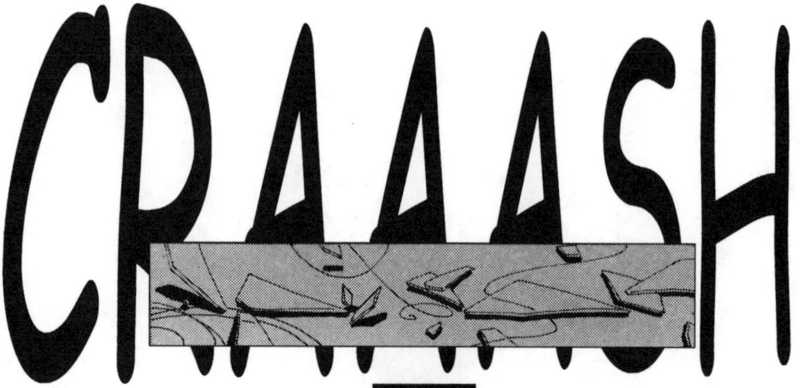
CRAAASH

『羽根』

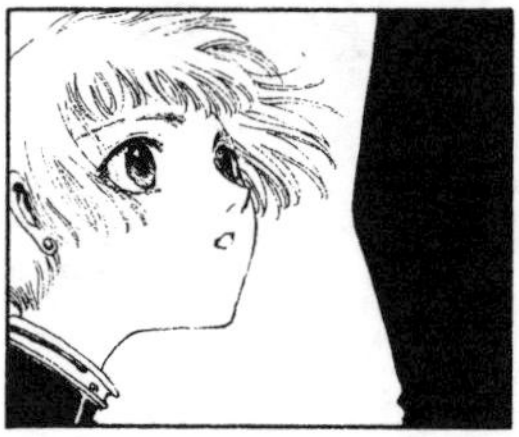

FEATHERS

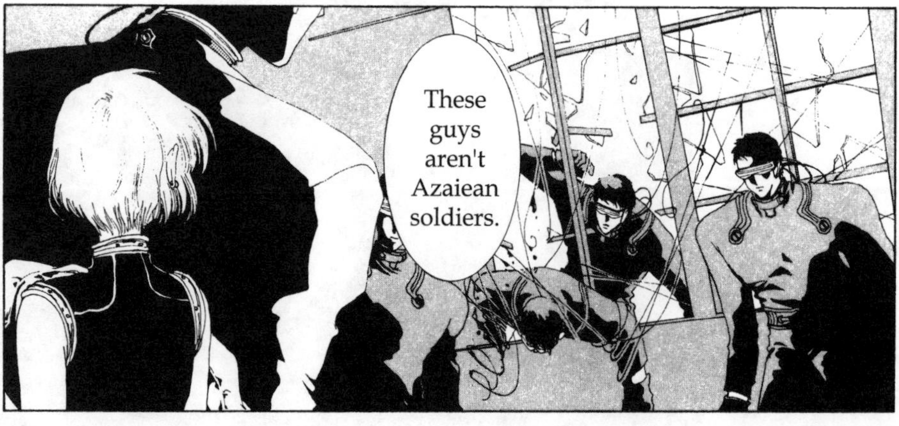
These guys aren't Azaiean soldiers.

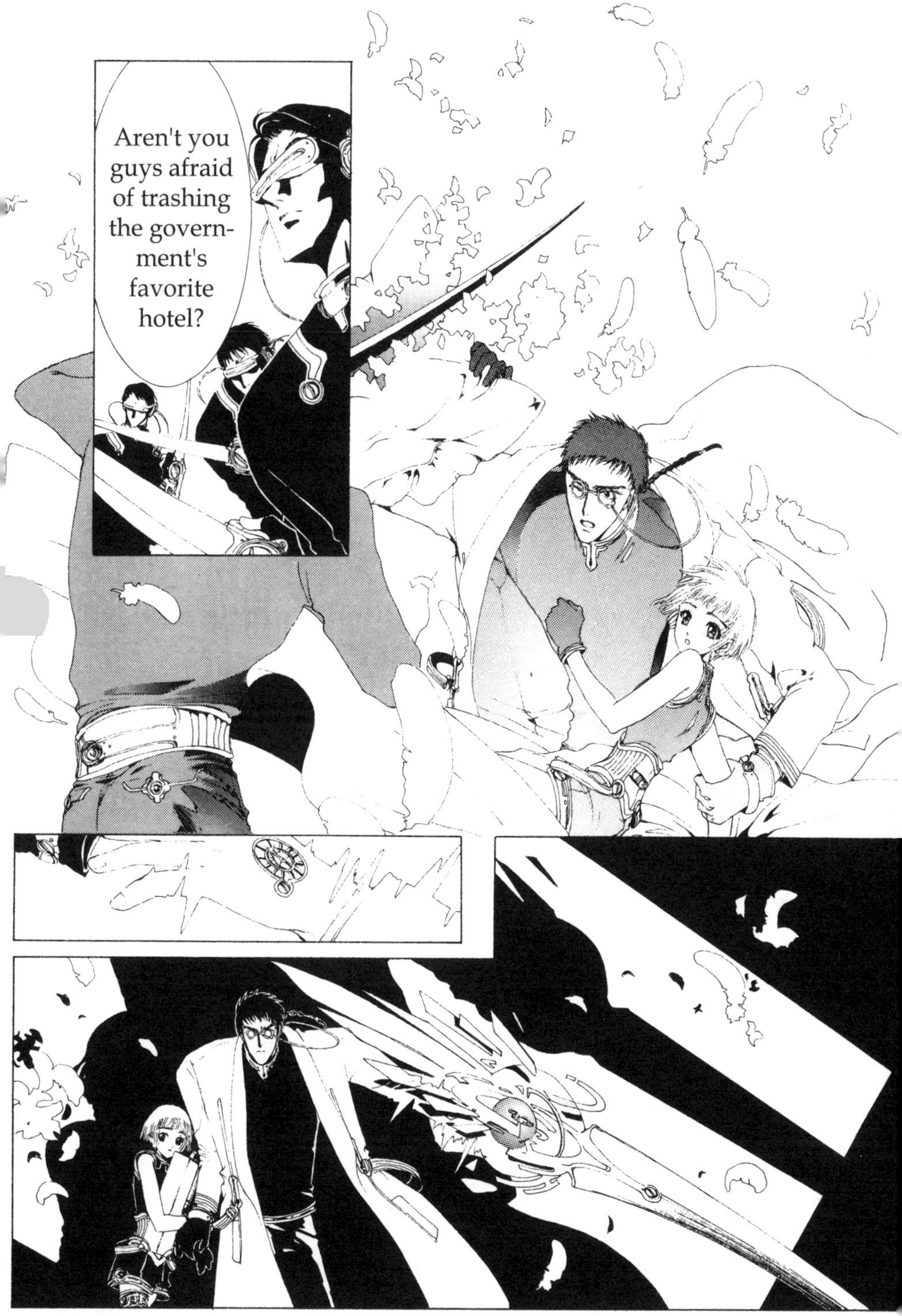
Aren't you guys afraid of trashing the government's favorite hotel?

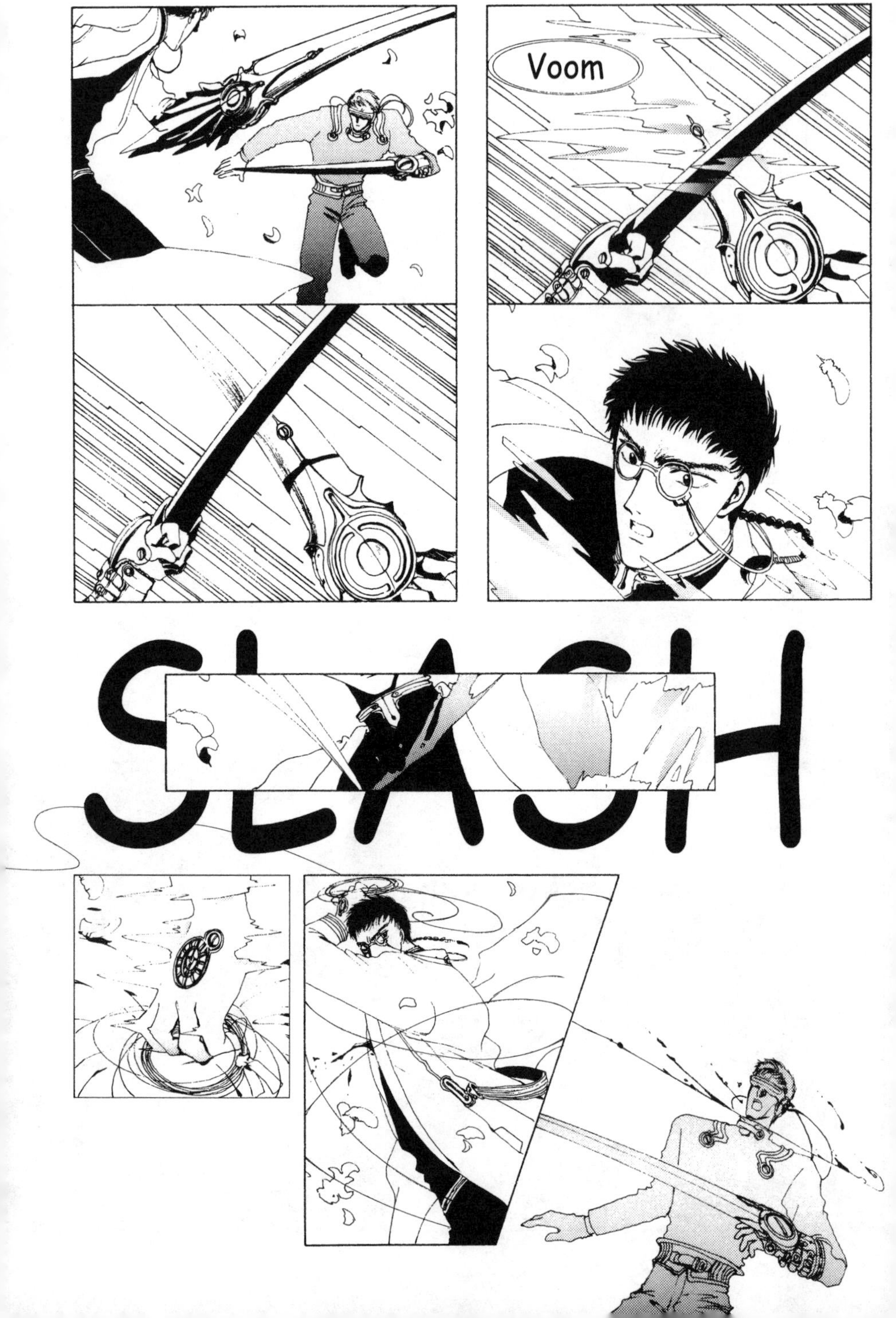
Voom
SLASH

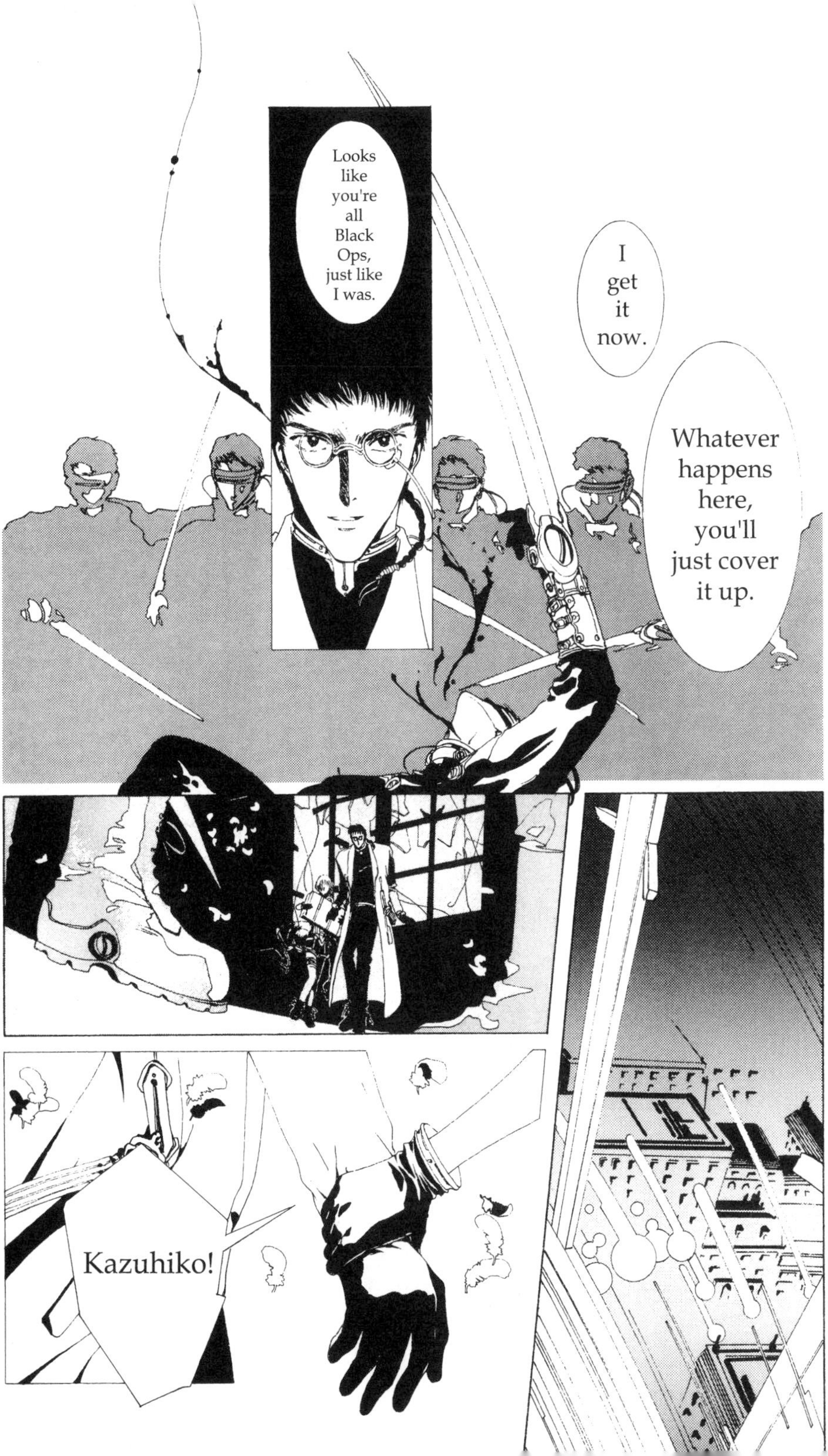
Looks like you're all Black Ops, just like I was.
I get it now.
Whatever happens here, you'll just cover it up.
Kazuhiko!

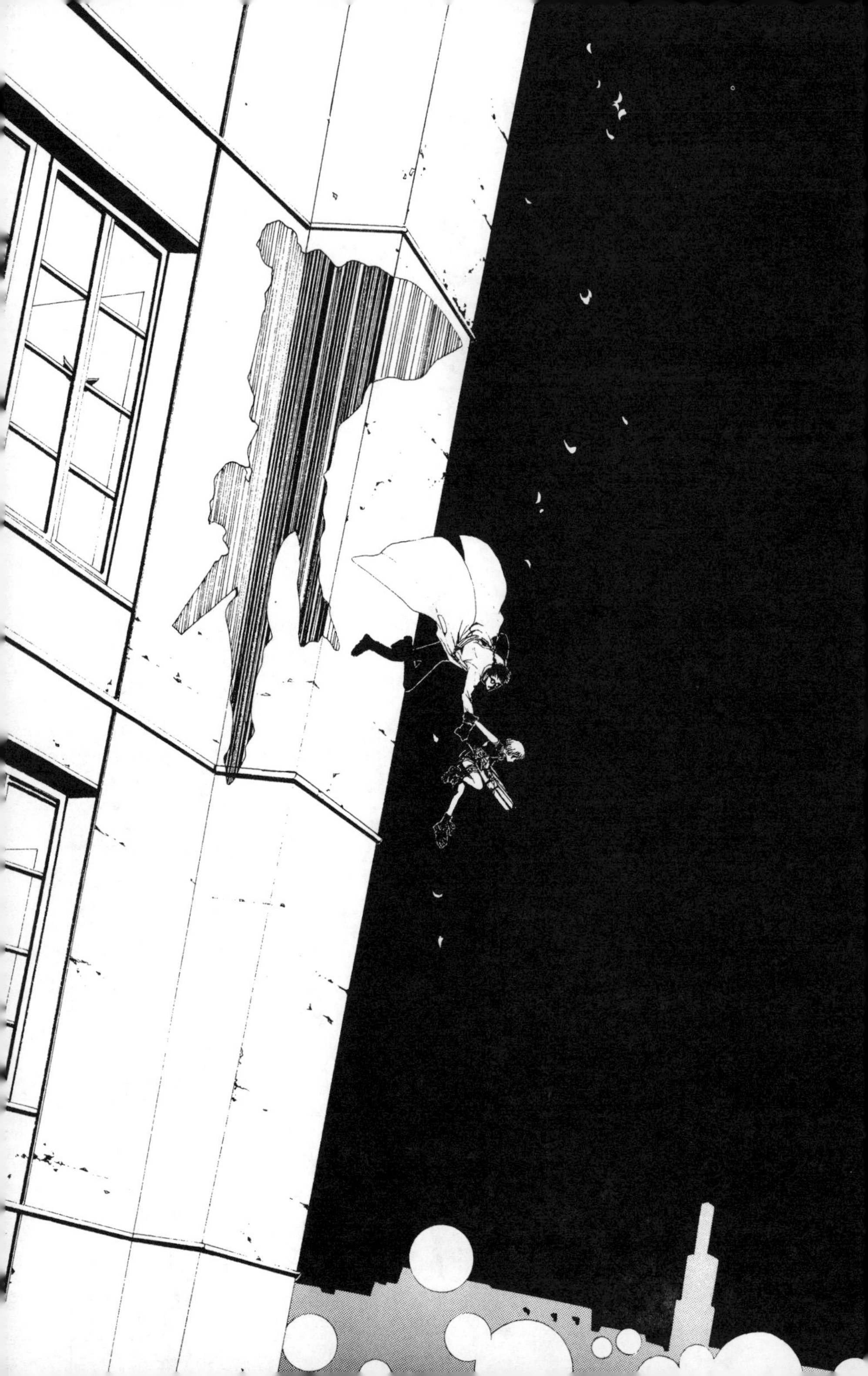

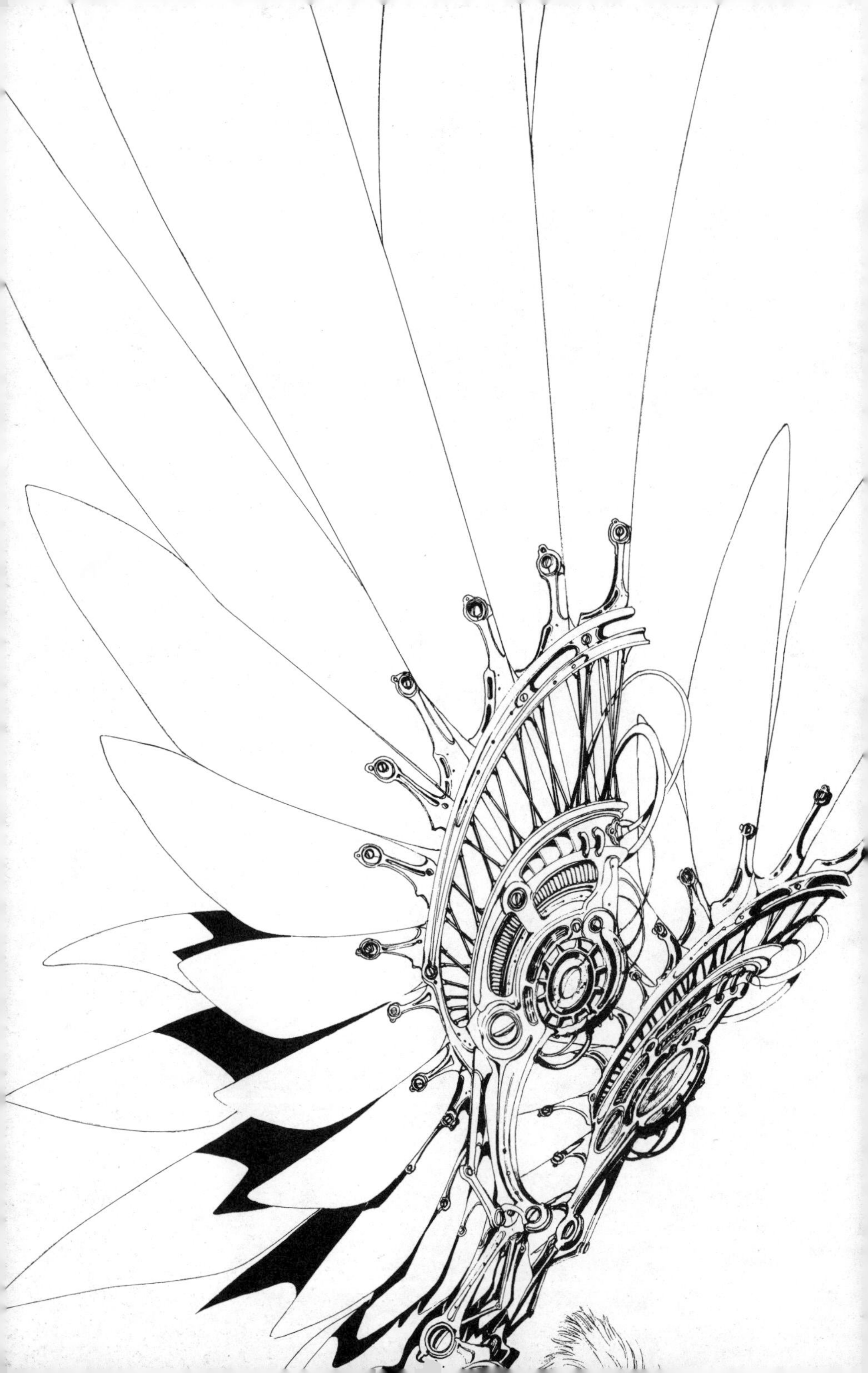

PLANNING+PRESENT+BOOK DESIGN

CLAMP

STORY

大川 七瀬
NANASE OHKAWA (CLAMP)

COMIC

もこな あぱぱ
MOKONA APAPA (CLAMP)

ASSISTANTS

五十嵐 さつき
SATSUKI IGARASHI (CLAMP)

猫井 みっく
MICK NEKOI (CLAMP)

LOGOTYPE・DIGITAL EFFECT

須子 博方
HIROMASA SUKO (P2)

冨岡 泰至
HIROSHI TOMIOKA (P2)

ENGLISH TRANSLATION

祖倉 哲人
TETSU TO SOKURA

EDITOR

山之内 秀樹
HIDEKI YAMANOUCHI (KODANSHA)

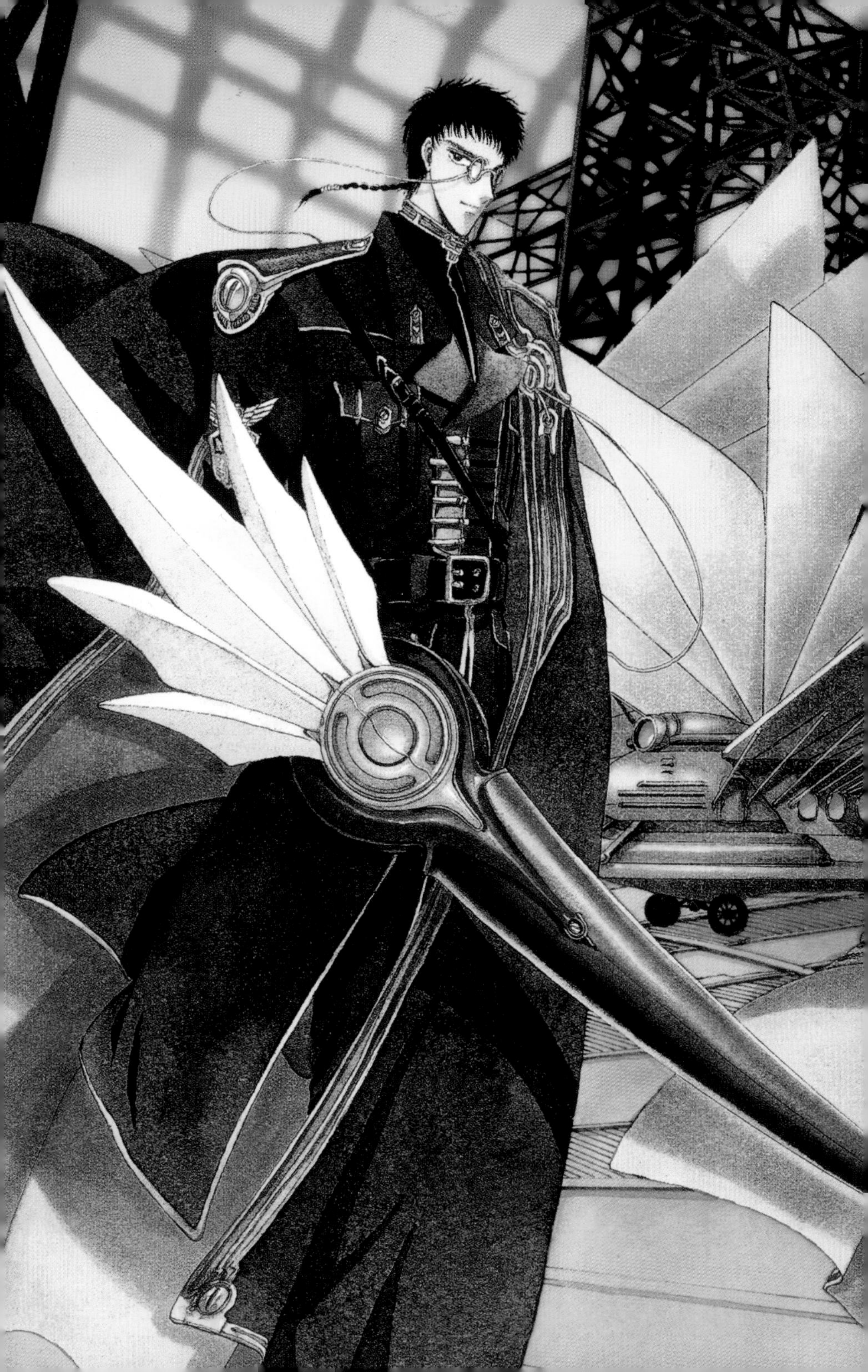

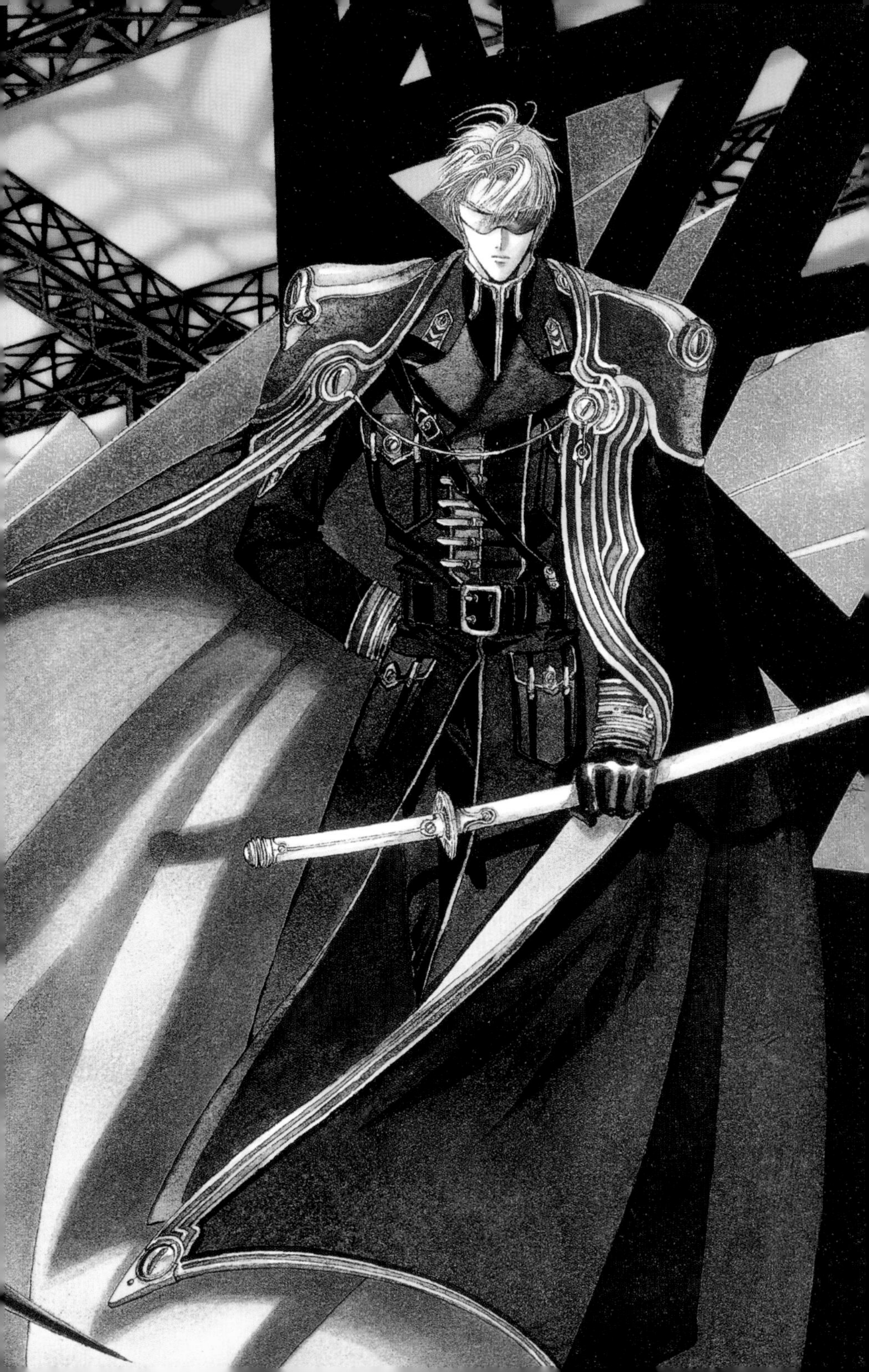

Clover 1 by CLAMP
TOKYOPOP is a registered trademark and
TOKYOPOP Manga is a trademark of Mixx Entertainment, Inc.
ISBN: 1-892213-66-4
First Printing May 2001

10   9   8   7   6   5   4   3   2   1

Clover 1 originally appeared in Smile Magazine No. 2.4 to No. 3.2 in their entirety.

Translator - Ray Yoshimoto.   Retouch Artist - Carol Concepcion.
Graphic Assistant - Steve Kindernay.   Graphic Designer - Akemi Imafuku.
Associate Editors - Jake Forbes, Katherine Kim.   Editors - Mary Coco, Michael Schuster.
Production Manager - Fred Lui.   Vice President of Publishing - Henry Kornman.

Email: editor@press.TOKYOPOP.com
Come visit us at www.TOKYOPOP.com.

TOKYOPOP
Los Angeles - Tokyo